SHINE
BRIGHT

SHINE BRIGHT

BRIGHT

60 DAYS to Becoming a Girl Defined by God

KRISTEN CLARK *and*

BETHANY BEAL

BakerBooks

a division of Baker Publishing Group
Grand Rapids, Michigan

© 2021 by Kristen Clark and Bethany Beal

Published by Baker Books
a division of Baker Publishing Group
PO Box 6287, Grand Rapids, MI 49516-6287
www.bakerbooks.com

Printed in the United States of America

Library of Congress Cataloging-in-Publication Data
Names: Clark, Kristen, 1987– author. | Beal, Bethany, 1988– author.
Title: Shine bright : 60 days to becoming a girl defined by God / Kristen Clark and Bethany Beal.
Description: Grand Rapids, Michigan : Baker Books, a division of Baker Publishing Group, [2021] | Includes bibliographical references. |
Identifiers: LCCN 2020042355 | ISBN 9781540901057 (cloth)
Subjects: LCSH: Young women—Religious life. | Young women—Prayers and devotions.
Classification: LCC BV4551.3 .C444 2021 | DDC 242/.633—dc23
LC record available at https://lccn.loc.gov/2020042355

21 22 23 24 25 26 27   7 6 5 4 3 2 1

Contents

Hey, sister!

It's wonderful to see you here! Somehow, someway, this book ended up in your hands, and we're so glad it did. This sixty-day devotional is designed to encourage you in your relationship with God and equip you to shine bright for His glory. Just like a lamp needs a power source to shine in the darkness, we need a power source to shine as well. When we spend time with God through prayer and reading His Word, we are empowered by His strength to shine bright for His glory in this dark world.

> Let your light shine before others, so that they may see your good works and give glory to your Father who is in heaven. (Matt. 5:16)

We encourage you to take a few extra minutes at the end of each devotional to dig deeper into the Scripture passages listed. The more you put into this devotional, the more you'll get out of it. The more you spend time with Jesus, the more you will understand how He wants you to reflect His image as a girl defined by God. Just keep in mind that this devotional isn't intended to replace your personal time in God's Word each day; it's meant to supplement it. We hope it's a great encouragement to you!

Cheering for you with love,
Kristen and Bethany

DAY 1

Where It All Starts

You are precious in my eyes,
and honored, and I love you.
Isaiah 43:4

We've all been there.

We walk into a room full of people, and we're convinced everyone's looking at us. Our thoughts start spinning . . .

Were they talking about me?

Do they think I look stupid?

Are they mad at me?

I (Kristen) know I'm not the only one who's faced this. If this experience is relatable to you as well, I've got great news: you don't have to keep wondering whether you're special enough, pretty enough, or "worth" being liked, talked to, and valued.

Before we go any further with this devotional, Bethany and I want you to know that a girl defined by God can walk into any room and be confident in who she is. If you decide to believe what God says about you, you can do that too.

Maybe you caught in the verse from Isaiah at the top of this page three words that God uses to describe His children, the Israelites. Those three words are a beautiful description of how God sees His children today.

Precious ... honored ... beloved.

How different would life be if we really believed those words described who we are as redeemed daughters of God?

Being a girl defined by God doesn't mean we'll never have an "Oh no! They're talking about me!" thought again. A God-defined girl just doesn't keep her focus on the "What if?" moments. She chooses to remember that she's precious, honored, and beloved. She embraces her true identity.

The Hebrew words God uses in Isaiah are powerful ones. God's children aren't just kinda loved, kinda special, kinda valued by Him. They're passionately cherished, loved unconditionally, and treasured so much that *nothing* can separate them from their true identity as His beloved children. If you've accepted Christ as your personal Savior, you are a child of God. Regardless of what other people have said or thought about you, it can't compete with God's truth.

In Matthew 5:16, Jesus tells us to "let [our] light shine before others." You and I were made to *shine bright* to reflect our amazing Savior. So ... will you choose to live in this truth today? What about every day?

This is where it all starts for a girl defined by God—our *identity*. When you're confident in what God says about you, honoring Him with your life and choices makes way more sense than doing things your own way. As you read the rest of this devotional, remember how loved, honored, and priceless you are. We're praying for you and believe God brought this book into your life for a reason. We can't wait to see what He'll do in your heart as we spend these sixty days together.

READY TO GO DEEPER? Read Isaiah 43:1–4 and Romans 8:35–39. What else does God say about His children's redeemed identity in these passages? What does He tell you about Himself? What is He inviting you to do with these truths?

DAY 2
Where It All Went Wrong

For all have sinned and fall short of the glory of God, and are justified by his grace as a gift, through the redemption that is in Christ Jesus.

Romans 3:23–24

Ever since I (Bethany) was a little girl, I've loved the sound of a basketball swishing through the net. I played basketball for *lots* of years, and I gotta tell you, the sound of a perfect shot going through the hoop is especially sweet if you're the one who nails the game winner.

Throughout all my years of playing, though, I missed countless shots. Realistically, I probably missed more shots than I made. Even professional athletes with a 40 percent shooting record are considered above average. That means they miss six out of every ten shots they take. That's a ton of misses.

What does all this basketball talk have to do with you? It's not just blah, blah, blah . . . sports info. The fact that *everyone*, even the pros, misses a lot of shots actually reveals something important about human nature. We all miss the mark. And— between you and me—in life, just like on the court, I miss the mark far more than I hit it.

In other words, I sin. I hurt people. I'm selfish. I fall short of God's glory, just like the verses at the top of this devotional describe. God's grace is my, and your, only hope in fighting sin.

The New Testament word for "sin" is *hamartia*, a term used by archers who miss their target. And beyond just missing a shot or one mark, sin misses the whole point of life, which is to glorify and honor God. That's why sin is never just about what we do; it's about *what we believe* and *who we are*. When we miss the mark by gossiping about friends or cheating on an exam or telling half-truths, we show God that His standard is less important to us than what we want.

The book of Romans also tells us that "the wages of sin is death, but the free gift of God is eternal life in Christ Jesus our Lord" (Rom. 6:23). In other words, God takes sin super seriously. At the very same time, He offers us the free gift of grace and eternal life in Jesus.

God knows that we can't hit the target without Him. He knows we're gonna miss the shot if we don't rely on His grace. That's why today's verses from Romans are such good news. Though we've all fallen short, we are justified through Christ's redemption.

If some of those words don't make sense to you, let me give you a couple details.

The word *justified* as a legal term means found innocent by a court of law. God, the rightful Judge, declared through Jesus that all the misses—all the sin—in your life won't be held against you; you are *justified* by His grace.

The word *redemption* is another term you won't hear too often in everyday life. Biblical redemption means winning or even buying back what was lost. Sin makes us *lost*. Redemption in Jesus means we're *found*. Redemption brings us back into right relationship with God, even though we've missed the mark again and again. Isn't that incredible?

It's important that we take sin as seriously as God does. That means even more seriously than a pro athlete takes her shooting percentage. God doesn't want us to be satisfied with hitting the mark only 40 percent of the time. He asks us to shoot for total holiness. Even though He understands we won't be completely perfect until He brings us home to heaven, He wants us to aim for the bull's-eye every time.

We're in this together, girl. I want to say no to sin and yes to God's gifts of grace, justification, and redemption. Will you say yes with me?

READY TO GO DEEPER? Read Galatians 2:20 and 2 Corinthians 5:21. What do these verses say about what God has done for you? What do they say about your life? How do you respond?

DAY 3
Love You to Life

God shows his love for us in that while we were still
sinners, Christ died for us.

Romans 5:8

People sometimes look at our books, blogs, and videos and think, *There's no way these girls would understand my problems; they've probably never done anything bad in their lives,* as if we're some kind of "super Christians" because we run a ministry.

We're gonna bust that myth right here, right now. Just like everyone else on this crazy planet, we both need the gospel *every single day.* We both wrestle with sinful hearts, but Jesus died for us. We are both enticed by sin, but Christ sacrificed His life for us. The moment of your worst struggle, the time you're most ashamed to remember, the situation you hoped no one would ever find out about is not only known to God, but He also chose to die for that sin.

The gospel is everything to us, and whether or not you know it, it's everything to you too. It's literally the difference between eternal life and eternal death.

You may be wondering at this point, *What exactly is the gospel?* Don't feel bad if you have this question! Girl, many churchgoers can't define the gospel, and we want to help change that.

The word *gospel* means "good news." When we use the word *gospel* we're referring to *the* good news, the good news that today's verse teaches: while we were still sinners, Christ died for us. When we encourage you to "share the gospel" with people who don't know Jesus yet, we mean for you to tell others that the God who loves them more than they can imagine gave His life for them even though He knows every sinful thing they've ever thought or done.

On first glance, the gospel doesn't seem like super good news to some people. The "while we were still sinners" part makes them mad. *I'm a good person! How dare anyone call me a sinner!*

If you're following this devotional in order, you already read that the Bible says *all* have fallen short of God's glory. Every single one of us has missed the mark (in other words, sinned). The gospel doesn't compare or quantify. Truth lumps us all together as people who need rescuing. We need a Savior who can rescue us from what's bent and broken inside, the part of us that hurts other people even though we don't understand why, the part that wants to lash out when we've been wronged, the part that does things we've promised ourselves we would never, ever do again. We need rescuing from our sin.

That's why the second part of the gospel—Christ died for us— is such a huge turn-everything-right-side-out truth. We love writing books about identity; we love teaching about God's amazing design for true beauty and femininity. At the heart of everything we do, though, is the amazing, life-changing truth that while we (Kristen, Bethany, and you!) have still sinned, Jesus died for us.

Never forget that if you've said yes to God's grace, you've been rescued and set free—forever. God loves you so much that nothing could stop Him from dying to save you. Remember, as a child of God, you are a precious, honored, and beloved daughter (Isa. 43:4). Though you have been lost, now you're found; though you've been guilty, you're innocent because of Jesus. That's incredible news, don't you think?!

READY TO GO DEEPER? One of our favorite Bible teachers wrote, "The gospel is this: We are more sinful and flawed . . . than we ever dared believe, yet at the very same time we are more loved and accepted in Jesus Christ than we ever dared hope."[1] Take a few minutes to journal, thanking God for rescuing you and praying for someone you know who doesn't yet believe in Jesus.

Finding Your Way

My sheep hear my voice, and I know them, and they follow me.

John 10:27

Driving through backwoods country roads without directions is not my idea of a fun day. I (Bethany) like to plan things out, have the map pulled up on my phone before I leave the house, and make sure I understand the basic route. I do *not* like feeling lost. Anyone relate? It's one of the worst feelings to have no idea where you are.

I had to learn the hard way that relying on my phone's GPS to get me where I'm going isn't an airtight plan.

Some friends and I were meeting up at a cool restaurant nestled in the Texas backwoods. It was a beautiful, meandering sort of drive past pastures full of cows (and more cows and *still more cows*). That's life in Texas! Everything was peachy until my phone just decided it was done cooperating. The maps app froze, and nothing I did brought it back to life. That pit-of-your-stomach sense of being lost gnawed at my insides.

I'm so grateful that I eventually made it to the restaurant that day. I'm even more grateful for the reminder this experience gave me. Doing life without directions is *not* how I want to live!

So many people wander around the roads of life without guidance. They bounce from place to place without a purpose or a sense of where they're headed next. Do you know anyone like this? Have you ever felt this way yourself?

I absolutely love that God doesn't leave us on our own, trying to figure out the best direction to take. It's a huge blessing to know that because Jesus saved me, the Holy Spirit is with me every moment. The verse for today's devotional, John 10:27, gives us two amazing promises: we can learn God's voice by reading His Word, and He will give us the directions we need as we follow Him.

Even without caller ID, you probably recognize certain people when they call. You know their voices so well that you automatically know who's on the other end of the line when you pick up. Maybe it's your best friend, a sibling, or one of your parents.

The Bible teaches that we can know God's voice, as spoken in His Word, in the same way we know the voices of the people we listen to most. You can probably guess where I'm headed with this. To know God's voice and get the directions you need, you gotta spend time studying His Word. That's why Kristen and I are such huge fans of daily time alone with God. Every day you spend reading His Word, learning how God speaks and what He says, makes you better able to discern His direction for your life.

Reading a devotional like this and digging into the daily Scripture passages mean you're already started on the right track. But don't stop there. By reading God's Word for yourself, you won't have to feel lost in the woods or anywhere else.[1]

READY TO GO DEEPER? Read John 14:6. Just like a map shows us the way to go, God's Word shows us *the* way. How does knowing that God's Word is the map for your life bring you encouragement? Journal your thoughts about it.

DAY 5

What Are You Afraid Of?

Fear not, for I am with you;
be not dismayed, for I am your God;
I will strengthen you, I will help you,
I will uphold you with my righteous right hand.

Isaiah 41:10

We live in a super anxious age. According to statistics, at least 75 percent of medical visits can be traced back to the effects of stress on the body.[1] When we're nervous or worried, every part of us suffers. We may experience headaches or stomach problems. We may feel like we can't catch our breath. Lots of people go to the doctor or emergency room with symptoms that feel like a heart attack but are actually the body's alarm signals designed to warn us that anxiety has burned too hot, too fast.

Nobody would sign up for this! Our hearts sincerely go out to everyone battling anxiety right now. We know how hard it is, especially for younger women. Did you know that women under twenty-five are most vulnerable to the negative impact of worry and fear? We'll spare you all the neurological details, but recent research shows how important it is that girls lower their anxiety and stress levels using healthy strategies (rather than zoning out with their phones).[2] Sister, the two of us have to do this as well, so we're in this fight together! But the awesome news is that there's truth that not only counterattacks but also totally *conquers* our fears. It's tucked inside Isaiah 41:10, the power-packed verse you read at the top of this devotional.

Though God's prophet Isaiah wrote these words thousands of years ago, he pinpointed some of the top fears women confess having.[3] He also gives us the hope we need to face them.

Women report feeling anxious about being alone or abandoned. God says, "Fear not, for I am with you." Sister, this is a *forever* promise! One of God's names is Emmanuel, which literally means "God with us." We are never, ever alone.

Women also say they're afraid that if people really knew them, they wouldn't be loved or accepted. But when God tells us, "Be not dismayed, for I am your God," He reminds us that He, the One who made us and knows every single thing about us, *fully* accepts us. Thanks be to Christ, we're fully accepted without the possibility of ever being rejected. We don't have to fear someone "finding us out." God knows and loves us right where we are.

The fear of losing control also plagues many of us. Keeping things under control has become our way to feel safe and secure. Trouble is, the more we try to control things, the more anxious we become. Isaiah 41:10 gives us hope! God promises to help us and strengthen us. He also promises to hold us up, above the wind and waves of our troubles.

And this brings us to one final (and huge!) fear women battle—the fear of failure. The word translated as *righteous* in Isaiah 41:10 also means "victorious" in Hebrew. God wins! The end of your story is victory, not defeat. There's no failure so big that it can alter God's ultimate victory over sin and death. As a daughter of the King, you're on the winning team. Victory is your birthright in Christ.

Next time you feel fear creeping in, remember God is with you and for you, strengthening you and securing your victory. Fear has to flee before our God!

READY TO GO DEEPER? Read Matthew 6:25–33. What does this passage teach about how God cares for you, His beloved girl? How can this help you face your worries and stresses? Journal about it!

DAY 6
Good, Good Father

See what great love the Father has lavished on us, that we should be called children of God! And that is what we are!

1 John 3:1[1]

The two of us know how blessed we are to have a great dad. He's an entrepreneur with an amazing work ethic; he's been a faithful husband to our mom for almost forty years; he lovingly raised all eight of us kids (yes, it's true: we're number two and number three of eight siblings!); and most importantly, he loves God.

What comes to your mind when you think of your dad? We know that answering that question is a lot easier for some people than for others. We started today's devotional with an acknowledgment of the gift we received—a gift we did nothing to earn or deserve—in having a great dad. But for some of you, hearing about a loving father, anyone's loving father, hurts.

If it were possible for us to reach through these pages and give you a huge hug right now, we would. The truth is, all of us have been wounded by our earthly fathers. Even though our dad is great, he's still disappointed us and let us down at times. We're well aware that he isn't perfect—and he's never pretended to be.

Maybe for you, though, it's almost impossible to imagine that a dad could be good or kind or loving. Or maybe you've never known your dad. Or maybe you thought you knew him, then everything changed.

No matter where you come from or what your dad is like, you have a heavenly Father who loves you lavishly. That's what 1 John 3:1, the verse at the top of this devotional, tells us. To "lavish" someone with love means to "give in excessive amounts and without limit." Your heavenly Father's love will never run out. It will always be more than enough. He will never fail you.

This love isn't simply a nice thing we can turn to when we're feeling low or need a little help—something like a divine boost in our smoothie. No way! Our heavenly Father's lavish love becomes our very identity; by it we are called His children. And because "the gifts and the calling of God are irrevocable" (Rom. 11:29), this love can never be taken away from us. No divorce can separate us from God, our Father. There is no possibility of abandonment with Him. "It is the LORD who goes before you. He will be with you; he *will not* leave you or forsake you. Do not fear or be dismayed" (Deut. 31:8, emphasis added). You need never doubt your heavenly Father. He keeps every one of His promises. That's why the book of Hebrews encourages, "Let us hold fast the confession of our hope without wavering, for he who promised is faithful" (Heb. 10:23).

We know how complicated the relationship with our earthly parents can be. We wish that, with one short devotional, we could heal any hurt you might have with your dad. Though that's not possible, here's what is . . . these words can turn your thoughts to how awesome your heavenly Father is. As you get to know

God the Father, the wounds of your past and present can be transformed by His never-stopping, never-giving-up, always-and-forever love. Spend some time with your heavenly Father today. He's ready to lavish you, His precious daughter, with love.

READY TO GO DEEPER? Read Matthew 10:29–31. What image does this passage use to describe God's love for you? How does it feel to know that He cares about you enough to number the hairs on your head? Talk to Him about it!

DAY 7
Would You Rather?

Finally, be strong in the Lord and in the strength of his might.

Ephesians 6:10

It's an oldie but a goodie: the "Would You Rather?" game. It's super simple but often hilarious and interesting.

The last time my friends and I (Bethany) played, this question came up: "Would you rather have shockingly overdeveloped muscles or have zero noticeable muscles and be a total wimp?"[1] Really weird but kinda intriguing question, right?

I'm not exaggerating when I report that every single person chose being überstrong. Being a wimp was appealing to 0.0 percent of us.

My friends were discussing physical strength, but strength can come in many different forms. And what one person values as a strength may not be as valued by someone else. Different kinds of strength are respected for particular reasons. Being a strong woman, for instance, can mean unique things to different girls.

There's a kind of strength that the Bible tells every one of us to seek. Did you catch it in the verse at the top of this page? Ephesians 6:10 commands, "Be strong in the Lord and in the strength of his might." Okay. But what on earth does that mean?

To begin, it means relying on God, not ourselves, as the source of our strength. While the world constantly tells people to "look inside," God promises that the greatest strength (in fact, the *only* reliable strength) comes from Him (read John 15:5 for more on this). Over and over, the Word declares that God is our strength, our hope, our security. Not sure? Here's a short list of verses that prove this point: Exodus 15:2; 1 Chronicles 29:11–12; Psalms 18:1–2 and 73:25–26; and Isaiah 40:29–31.

Being strong "in the strength of his might" also means remaining *in* God's strength, united with Jesus. The Bible has another word for this—*abiding*—which is fancy for "being at home in."[2] As you grow closer to God, you become more at home in His strength. For most people, being at home means being comfortable, knowing your way around, feeling at ease. Being at home in God's strength—"in the strength of his might"—means you're able to operate within and even be at ease with God's power in and through you. You don't fight against Him; you don't want to go on your own. Unity with Jesus is your secret to success.

Commentators have explored much more in regard to this verse, and we encourage you to dig even deeper! We'd like to leave you with just one more thing for today: because you belong to God, the same power our heavenly Father displayed when He raised Jesus from the grave is in you. Ephesians 6:10 promises this! One of the Greek words for "strength of his might," *kratos*, is also used to describe God's power in bringing Jesus back to life.[3] Literally *nothing* can come against this strength.

You know what this means? Because of Christ, you and I have greater spiritual strength than we can possibly comprehend. Let's start living like this is true! We're not weak girls trying to look for "power within." In Christ, we're *kratos* strong, and nothing can stand against us.

READY TO GO DEEPER? If you haven't already, look up the verses listed in this devo. Journal about this: What would it look like for God's power to flow through you in daily life?

Not Some, But *All*

If we confess our sins, he is faithful and just to forgive us our sins and to cleanse us from all unrighteousness.

1 John 1:9

I (Kristen) stood outside my parents' door, palms sweating, stomach churning. I felt ill. Weak. Afraid.

I knew I needed their help. I was tired of fighting my sin alone. I believed what God said in the Bible: "Whoever conceals his transgressions will not prosper, but he who confesses and forsakes them will obtain mercy" (Prov. 28:13). I desperately needed that mercy, but this was one of the hardest moments of my life.

As a teen, this secret sin had been plaguing me for some time. My sexual desires and the things I did to satisfy my own lustful passions were hurting me spiritually. That much was obvious. But tell my parents? *Really?*

Then I remembered the words from James 5:16, "Confess your sins to one another and pray for one another, that you may be healed. The prayer of a righteous person has great power as it is working." I knew my parents were godly people. I knew their prayers could help me. I knew that they would love me no matter what.

I knocked. I told them about my struggles. I cried . . . a lot. And my healing journey began.

No matter what sin you've battled or are battling, freedom starts with confession. And confession leads to forgiveness. That's why our verse for the day, 1 John 1:9, is so hopeful. Its promise is huge. If we confess our sins, God is faithful and just to forgive all our sin and cleanse us from everything that's contaminated us.

Did you catch the essential word *all* in this verse? God doesn't forgive us for some things and make us work for others. He doesn't cleanse us from part of our sin and leave the residue as a reminder that we should never do it again. He totally, completely forgives us when we confess and repent. Both Bethany and I love to use Psalm 51:10 as a prayer of confession and repentance: "Create in me a clean heart, O God, and renew a right spirit within me." I encourage you to memorize it, like we have, so that when you realize sin has you moving in the wrong direction, God's Word can get you back on the right path.

You may not have an open door like I did to talk to your parents about the secret sin in your life. But you can still bring things into the light with trusted, godly support—maybe it's a church leader, a mentor, or a Christian teacher or professor. Don't let secret sin break you like I did for so long! Find the mercy that Jesus is ready to give when we confess, repent, and receive the pure, clean heart God's forgiveness provides.

Before you take it, the first step of confession feels terrifying. But, sister, I promise . . . that step is *so, so freeing*. It's totally understandable if you feel nervous. You know I did! But if God can give me the strength to be brave, He can give it to you too.

With the promise of *all* (i.e., perfect cleansing, perfect forgiveness, perfect acceptance) in front of us, we can do this together.[1] And if you want to learn more about how to battle sexual sin specifically, check out our book *Sex, Purity, and the Longings of a Girl's Heart.*

READY TO GO DEEPER? Is there a particular sin you can't seem to conquer? Write a prayer confessing it to God and thanking Him for the gift of forgiveness. Then ask Him to bring to mind a godly person you can confess your sin to and ask to pray with and for you.

Will You Ever Be Satisfied?

For he satisfies the longing soul,
and the hungry soul he fills with good things.

Psalm 107:9

My younger sister baked the most delicious cookies one afternoon, and I (Bethany) just had to have one. As she pulled them out of the hot oven, the sweet smell of baked sugar and dark chocolate wafted through the air. Mmm . . . I just wanted one little bite. One little taste.

Right. Who can take one bite of a delicious, freshly baked cookie and stop there?

After I promptly consumed three full cookies, I felt happy and satisfied. With the rich chocolate flavor lingering on my tongue, I went about the rest of my day feeling pretty satisfied. That's all I needed. Just a few bites.

But then I woke up the next day, and guess what? I had a serious case of the munchies. I was craving another bite of those delicious dark chocolate chip cookies! My initial satisfaction had worn off completely. All I craved was another little bite. *Just one more.*

Can you relate?

We all ache to be satisfied. Every single one of us.

As women, we think this new thing (the perfect skin product) or that change (losing some weight) will finally bring satisfaction. And it may—for a moment. But there's a reason chasing satisfaction has been compared to chasing the wind. People mostly end up with a whole lotta nothing.

The story can be different for those who place their faith in Jesus Christ. Unlike the momentary pleasure of a cookie, He fills the hungry soul "with good things" (Ps. 107:9). Why doesn't everyone jump at this opportunity? Who in their right mind would reject being totally satisfied with good things from God?

Apparently, a lot of us aren't in our right minds. We look for satisfaction at the gym, in relationships, at school or work, and yes, even in the kitchen, but rarely in the One who alone can truly satisfy (see Ps. 63:1–5). Still, God calls to us:

> Come, everyone who thirsts,
>   come to the waters;
> and he who has no money,
>   come, buy and eat!
> Come, buy wine and milk
>   without money and without price.
> Why do you spend your money for that which is not
>   bread,
>   and your labor for that which does not satisfy?
> Listen diligently to me, and eat what is good,
>   and delight yourselves in rich food.
> Incline your ear, and come to me;
>   hear, that your soul may live. (Isa. 55:1–3)

Sister, you can make a huge decision today. Will you spend your money, time, effort, and energy on what truly satisfies, or will you chase after the wind? The default choice is to go the world's way by pursuing momentary pleasures. But that doesn't have to be your story.

To find satisfaction, to be filled with the good things God promises, we need to obey what Isaiah 55 teaches: listen diligently. The prophet warns, "Hear, that your soul may live" (v. 3). He urges us to tune in to what God says and tune out the messages of the world. The life of your soul and the satisfaction of your heart are at stake. It's not easy to keep our ears attuned to God's messages when the world is screaming at us from every direction. It takes diligence, just like this passage says. But consider the reward: you will be deeply satisfied. Long after the chocolate has melted in your mouth, you will be *filled*. If you ask me, that's a prize worth fighting for.

READY TO GO DEEPER? Read Psalm 63. How does the psalmist describe being satisfied by the Lord? Write your own description of being totally satisfied by good things in Jesus.

DAY 10
What's in Your Heart?

The good person out of the good treasure of his heart produces good, and the evil person out of his evil treasure produces evil, for out of the abundance of the heart his mouth speaks.

Luke 6:45

I (Kristen) remember it so clearly. A few girlfriends and I were chatting about our mutual friend's upcoming wedding. At some point the conversation headed south.

"I just didn't think someone as beautiful as her should marry such an unattractive guy."

Other friends chimed in for a bit, some agreeing that it was "really weird" and they "couldn't understand it either." Then, to my relief, the topic shifted.

It took me a while to figure out why this conversation bothered me so much. Ultimately, I was ashamed to realize that I'd actually had similar thoughts about other dating or engaged couples. I may not have said these things out loud, but I had certainly let them run through my brain. I felt ashamed.

I don't want you to miss the important but tough lesson I learned from this conversation. Our words reflect what's already inside us. That's what Jesus meant when He spoke our verse for the day: "Out of the abundance of the heart [your] mouth speaks"

(Luke 6:45). According to Jesus, things don't just pop out of our mouths, despite the popular excuses people use when they say something hurtful. "I don't know where that came from! It just came out." Not so much, Jesus tells us.

When I verbally tear someone down or gossip, I'm bringing to the surface what's already deep within me. Yikes! That's terrible. This means that if I'm gossiping about a friend's struggles—even if it appears as though I'm sharing the details so someone else can pray—I'm actually breathing into the world the selfish desire for "hot tea" that's already in me. I don't want that!

Many of us struggle with using our words well.[1] In fact, gossip is a sin to which many Christians turn a blind eye. But God doesn't want us to "discuss" (which often equals ripping apart) the people we follow on social media. He's not okay with us tearing others down to make ourselves feel better. There's no way He's cool with girls talking about one another behind their backs or treating people one way in person and treating them horribly behind the scenes.

Thankfully, God offers us a far better way forward! He teaches us the following:

> Without wood a fire goes out;
>> without gossip a quarrel dies down. (Prov. 26:20)[2]

Without our words, the fire of spreading news will burn out. In other words, at times it's best to simply shut our mouths! The book of Proverbs reminds us of this:

> When words are many, transgression is not lacking,
>> but whoever restrains his lips is prudent. (10:19)

When in doubt, just zip it! This is something I'm still consciously trying to practice every day.

Pray with me that God will purify our hearts from the inside out. That way, when our words come out, they'll reflect a heart of beauty and kindness. Sister, I know it's a challenge to use your words well. I'm right there with ya! But the Bible is clear: "Death and life are in the power of the tongue" (Prov. 18:21). Speak life, and you'll change the world, one word at a time.

READY TO GO DEEPER? Here's a prayer from Psalm 141:3 to memorize:

> Set a guard, O LORD, over my mouth;
>   keep watch over the door of my lips!

DAY 11

I'm Craving . . .

So put away all malice and all deceit and hypocrisy and envy and all slander. Like newborn infants, long for the pure spiritual milk, that by it you may grow up into salvation— if indeed you have tasted that the Lord is good.

1 Peter 2:1–3

Every holiday season a craving erupts within the two of us. Coffee shops and restaurants alike tempt us with the siren song of creamy, chocolaty goodness. Girl, it's a lot easier to resist the call during a hot-enough-to-fry-an-egg-on-my-car Texas summer. But once the sweaters, scarves, and beanies come out, both of us are sorely tempted to become absolute fanatics, to throw out our health and financial wisdom for one thing: café mochas. The struggle is real!

Have you ever had a strong craving? Like a certain-week-every-month-I-must-have-french-fries kind of craving?

Cravings are real physical signals that your body picks up. One challenge is that our bodies don't always interpret or understand the true nature of its cravings. For instance, scientists have shown that while people crave cold, sugary treats during the summer (think ice cream or shaved ice), the body is actually crying out for water. Dehydration can cause us to crave something that won't actually satisfy us.[1]

In a fascinating way, we see the same thing happen in people's spiritual lives. The soul sends out signals. We need time with God—time to be loved, guided, and convicted. But like a kid who turns away a water bottle in favor of an ice-cream cone, we choose to stream, scroll, or shop instead. Just as ice cream isn't bad (in our humble opinion, it's actually a fabulous gift from God), entertainment and shopping can be fun too. That said, they're not *necessary* to our very existence the way water and time with Jesus are. To help our bodies and souls crave what actually satisfies, we need to feed higher cravings and starve lower ones.

That's, in part, what our verses for today teach. Peter encourages us to "long for" (the Greek word can also be translated "crave") "pure spiritual milk." A quick review of commentaries on this passage reveals that pure spiritual milk refers to the solid, untainted doctrine of God's Word. A steady diet of God's perfect Word—which gives life, direction, and hope—makes our souls strong and resilient. We feed this craving by indulging in and enjoying Bible study, fellowship with other Christians who sharpen us in faith, and personal times of worship.

If these are the higher cravings we're called to feed, what are the lower cravings we need to starve? According to this passage, we should starve longings for "malice and all deceit and hypocrisy and envy and all slander." While this isn't an exhaustive list, it gives us some biggies to start working on: pretending and finessing, comparison and jealousy, anger and clapbacks. Putting our different cravings next to one another, it's clear which things are going to help and which will hurt. Sadly, we so often get tricked into satisfying lower cravings because the mindlessness of browsing our social media feeds keeps us from seeing clearly.

Here's a step you can take today: ask God to increase your hunger for His Word. Stop right now and pray that He'll make your craving for His living water stronger than your longing for anything else. We'll do the same!

READY TO GO DEEPER? Read Matthew 5:6. What does God promise as a gift to those who crave higher things? What does *righteousness* mean? Look it up in an online Bible dictionary and journal about what you find.[2]

As We Forgive Those . . .

Be kind to one another, tenderhearted, forgiving one another, as God in Christ forgave you.

Ephesians 4:32

I (Kristen) love, love, *love* Zack Clark. I waited three (long and agonizing) years for him to initiate a dating relationship. Walking down the aisle toward Zack—looking extremely handsome in his tux—was an experience like no other. This was *it*, the moment I'd been imagining for years. I was starting the rest of my life with the man of my dreams (it's totally cool if you sigh romantically right now).

Being married to Zack has been out-of-this-world amazing. I love his heart for God. I love how smart he is. I love how he cherishes me. I'm telling you, I love this guy. That's probably why it was so hard for me to realize, after we had been married only a short time, that I didn't always *act* lovingly toward him. Ugh! Marriage showed me that I'm not nearly as kind, tenderhearted, and forgiving as I'd hoped (maybe even thought?) I was.

Trust me. Whether you are single or have been married a long time, one of the most important things you and I can do is learn to forgive like Jesus forgives—quickly, lovingly, and completely, over and over again.

You and I both know it's not always easy to forgive. Sometimes the people who hurt us have no clue what they did. Some people never say they're sorry for the awful things they've done. Others don't care how we feel; they actually *want* to hurt us.

Sadly, I've been on both sides of these scenarios. Yeah, I've been hurt before . . . and badly. I've also held back from seeking reconciliation because I wanted the other person to know what they did was *way* worse than what I did. I've wounded people unintentionally. And—this one really stings—I've deliberately sinned against people I love, even Zack, when I've been at my worst.

To sum things up, I need forgiveness from Jesus, and I also need Jesus's help to forgive the people who have hurt me. You need forgiveness and help forgiving too. We all do.

Today's verse encourages us to be kind and tenderhearted. This means cultivating a softness, rather than a sharpness, in our hearts. It means loving so much that we risk getting hurt. That may sound kinda scary, but that's how Jesus loves us. Since we're called to love as Jesus loves, we're also called to show kindness—even to people who have hurt us.

Note: this doesn't mean we have to let people keep hurting us! We can set up healthy boundaries and be wise in our relationships. What it *does* mean, though, is that we choose kindness rather than bitterness in our hearts. We choose not to poison ourselves with unforgiving thoughts. Girl, nobody gets hurt more than you when you choose to hold on to unforgiveness. Believe me; I've been there.

The other part of this verse says we should forgive as God, in Christ, forgives us. Basically, we have a choice to make. Either be like Him and forgive or refuse His help and choose the path of bitterness. There's no third option, like "I'll just ignore that" (yeah right) or "I'll forget what they did and move on" (fails every time). Instead, we're called to forgive like God forgives us in Jesus. He *chooses* to forgive.

Sometimes we choose to forgive, and there's instant joy and reconciliation. Other times we have to choose forgiveness over many years (with hurts like abuse, this is often the case). This doesn't mean we forget what happened; it means we choose to release the offender into God's hands. We choose never to bring up their offense in a condemning way.

Today's verse shows we *can* forgive. We *can* be set free from bitterness. God never tells you to do something He doesn't give you the power to do. So, choose forgiveness, and His kindness and tenderheartedness will start flowing out of you, even to those who've hurt you.[1]

READY TO GO DEEPER? Read John 13:34–35 to see how Jesus's love changes us and the whole world too. Spend some time journaling about someone you need to forgive, asking for God's help and receiving it.

DAY 13

Better to Be Speechless

Let no corrupting talk come out of your mouths, but only such as is good for building up, as fits the occasion, that it may give grace to those who hear.

Ephesians 4:29

My dad and I (Bethany) had just finished our breakfast and walked to the counter to pay our bill. The girl at the cash register stared at me for a few seconds, then came out with something I wasn't anticipating: "Wow! You're freakishly tall."

Umm . . .

The worldly part of me might have relished skewering her with a clapback like, "Wow! You're freakishly rude," but that's not what I said. I honestly don't remember exactly how I responded. My mind was already spinning on what a great story this would make for our sisterhood.

What on earth do you do when people say rude, unkind, or flat-out dumb things to you? It has happened to all of us more than once!

If you're going through this devotional in order, a couple days ago you read a devo from Kristen about how you can use your own words well. You also read about the importance of forgiving the people who hurt you. Today I want to challenge you to consider two godly strategies that can help you stay away from the sarcastic word grenades you might want to lob at someone who calls you, I don't know, something "freakish."

Our verse for today comes from Ephesians, an encouraging and practical book that touches on a wide variety of topics, including the importance of our words. Ephesians 4:29 tells us we should not allow poisonous (corrupting) words to come out of our mouths. This also means we shouldn't allow lies to take root in our hearts. When someone makes a hurtful and untrue comment about us, the most important thing we can do is speak biblical truth to ourselves: "That lie isn't from God. I choose not to believe it. Instead, I embrace God's identity for me."

Of course, doing this in the middle of a conversation may not work. But whether you tell yourself the truth immediately or later, it's important that you reject and replace the corrupting words that want to get into your brain. Otherwise they'll end up nesting in there, taking root, poisoning your thinking, and then coming out as hurtful words to someone else.

Strategy #1: Speak biblical truth to yourself and repeat as many times as necessary.

Strategy #2: Respond with gracious words that—as our verse says—build up. The Greek term here means "constructive." In other words (pun totally intended), let God use your words to help others. What you say then becomes a gift of grace.

How might this have looked in my checking-out-after-breakfast story? Maybe I would have replied, "Yeah, being tall has always been something that's made me different from other girls. I've had some pretty big insecurities in my life, and that's why I'm super passionate about helping other girls understand that their identity comes from Jesus, who created each of us to look unique. Have you ever felt insecure about something?"

This could have turned the whole conversation into an opportunity to witness, to find out about struggles she might have battled. There's no guarantee she would've responded kindly, but I would've reversed the hurtfulness of her comment in my own heart. See what I mean?

I know this isn't easy. It's tough to respond in a godly way to someone else's "corrupt" commentary. But here's the thing: you remove the sting of their poisonous word darts when you tell yourself the truth and respond with grace. I'd rather have peace than poison in my brain. Wouldn't you?

READY TO GO DEEPER? Read Proverbs 15:1. How can this verse apply to heated conversations where corrupt words are flying this way and that?

Accepted without Exception

Therefore welcome one another as Christ has welcomed you, for the glory of God.

Romans 15:7

You know those notifications that pop up when someone connects with you on social media?

(Insert digital sound here.) "Grace has accepted your friend request." Yes!

That always feels super good, right?

Feeling accepted is huge. Actually *being* accepted is even huger.

Every girl I know craves acceptance. Not feeling accepted drives people to do crazy things, whereas confidence in your level of acceptedness is like pure gold. You know what I'm talkin' about!

What if we could—once and for all—answer the question of whether we're accepted? Do you think it might make a difference for our day-to-day lives if we knew that we were accepted without exception?

When we tell girls they are always and forever going to be accepted, they have a hard time believing it. That's totally relatable, since our world is all about being accepted one minute and rejected another. You're invited to this and left out of that, part of them but then kicked to the curb. It's exhausting.

We want to invite you to a better way: receive your welcome in Jesus, and extend it to every other person you know. In case that sounds a little confusing, let's break it down.

Our verse for the day, from Romans 15:7, urges us to "welcome one another as Christ has welcomed you." The word *welcome* here can also be translated "accepted." In other words, Romans 15:7 promises that Jesus accepts you. Period. No ifs or buts.

And because you have been accepted by Jesus, you are "in" with God the Father and God the Holy Spirit in the exact same way. You are accepted without the possibility of rejection. You can now accept others in the same way—totally, freely, and joyfully.

A sad but major reason girls reject each other is they're afraid that, if everyone else is accepted, there won't be a place for them. Someone has to be "out" for there to be an "in" crowd, right? Wrong! At least not when it comes to eternity (which is, let me remind you if you haven't thought about it in a while, *a whole lot longer* than now).

You have the ability to turn this world into a far more loving one. The more you welcome and accept others, the more Jesus's love spreads throughout the world. Isn't that an awesome thought? Instead of being one of the rejecters in this world, be a girl who pursues and accepts like Jesus does.

And enjoy your own acceptance in Him. Embrace it! In most schools or workplaces, being in with the right person can seal your position in any group. That's totally true of the spiritual world. You are in with Jesus, which means you're in . . . always . . . everywhere . . . for eternity.

READY TO GO DEEPER? Read James 2:1–4. What does the Bible teach about accepting some people more than others? Does God play favorites? Read Romans 2:11 to discover the Bible's answer.

DAY 15

Gonna Build You Up

"All things are lawful," but not all things are helpful.
"All things are lawful," but not all things build up.

1 Corinthians 10:23

Once upon a time, I (Bethany) did a super foolish thing.

I was young and insecure about my pale skin. Looking at gorgeously tanned models and other people whose skin couldn't be compared to fresh dairy cream, I came up with what was—in my young and naïve mind—a perfect plan. I would simply lie in the sun for several hours, and my skin would become browned and beautified.

Sunscreen was not part of this plan.

Yeah. You can imagine how well this went down. After a couple hours fully exposed to the sun's intense Texas rays, I was fried. Girl, I was FRIED.

Like so full-on-blistering-skin fried that I still—years later— have damaged skin on the front of my legs. All that sun exposure didn't make me more beautiful. It made me vulnerable and injured.

Let's be clear that the sun itself didn't hurt me. The sun's rays aren't always harmful. But we all know that exposing ourselves to the sun in the wrong ways leads to crummy consequences and unnecessary pain. (Spending hours in the sun without sunscreen? Seriously bad idea.)

The same thing is true of our media exposure. Media isn't inherently bad; I love chilling to a good movie or listening to a fun song as much as the next girl. In fact, media is an amazing gift. I wouldn't have met many of the women in the GirlDefined Sisterhood without the Internet, and I'm super grateful that we can use media to honor God in lots of ways, including having fun.

That said, if I use media in the wrong ways—basically overexposing myself to its harmful "rays"—I'm gonna get fried. And the damage may last a *long* time. The same is true for you.

Here are some examples: You may have been shown or sent an image that you just *can't* get out of your head, no matter how hard you've tried. You may have read a comment or a whole book that seriously impacted you (and not for the better). You may have seen a TV show, movie, music video, or even a commercial that's now on a repeating loop in your brain. You may have listened to a song many times before you realized what it was actually saying, and now you're stuck with lyrics that don't help you be a girl after God's heart. My friend, this is all relatable. Media can do this . . . and more.

Our verse for today is a great way to measure whether the media rays we're being exposed to are harmful. First Corinthians 10:23 tells us that everything, including using media, may be lawful, but not everything is *helpful*. If we allow this truth to sink down into our hearts, we'll have a way better gauge of what media we should keep and what we should ditch.

So that's your challenge for today: write down the last ten to twenty movies or TV shows you watched; songs you listened to; sites you visited; blogs, books, or posts you read, etc. Write *spiritually helpful* or *spiritually hurtful* next to each one. It's okay if this takes some time. It will only work if you're honest. And if you are, you'll be able to see whether you're on the way to being (or are already) fried by your media usage or you're staying safe. Don't let yourself get burned unnecessarily by media rays. You have the choice, my friend.

READY TO GO DEEPER? Read 1 Corinthians 6:12. What does the apostle Paul teach us can happen if we go ahead with things that don't build us up? Pray for God's help to see clearly today.

What Are You Looking At?

The LORD sees not as man sees: man looks on the outward appearance, but the LORD looks on the heart.

1 Samuel 16:7

I (Kristen) turned around in front of my bedroom mirror, eager to see the full effect of my new jeans. Not gonna lie, this thought crossed my mind: *You look seriously hot.* My grueling workout schedule had definitely paid off as my jeans sat perfectly snug on my waist and hips. I felt powerful . . . alluring . . . even seductive. On my way to meet friends that night, I was excited that guys might notice me. And they did. Feeling desired and in control had never felt so good.

Even though I look back at that teenage me and wince a bit, I also understand what I was really looking for: I wanted to be wanted. I wanted to be seen. I wanted to be loved. I was just going about it in a completely backward way.

We all want to be noticed and affirmed. And this isn't actually the problem. The problem is that our world tells us we should use our feminine beauty to get the affirmation we crave.

Our verse for today, 1 Samuel 16:7, presents a far different picture. From it we learn that God looks at the heart, not at the outward appearance. As girls defined by God, we're called to be like Him in every way, to be set apart—pure and holy—just like He is. If God looks at the heart (i.e., inner character), rather than the outward appearance, don't you think we should too?

How crazy would it be if, today, the whole world went completely dark? No one could see what they or anyone else looked like. It might be easier to "see" who people really are. We might look past what doesn't matter and focus on what really does. We'd be a lot more like God, I think.

As you know, however, the whole world is *not* dark, and the sun will continue to shine. So, how do we practically navigate looking at the heart rather than the outward appearance?

One of the best ways we can do this is by celebrating others. Intentionally thinking about and pointing out great things about other people is a fantastic way to honor God (after all, He created the person you're complimenting). It also builds others up, as God's Word encourages us to do (see Eph. 4:29 for more on this).

Celebrating others doesn't just have to end with giving people compliments on their appearance (though it's never gonna hurt to tell the cashier at your grocery store that she has beautiful eyes or that the dress a friend chose for church looks really nice on her). Go beyond just the outward appearance, like God does, and celebrate the Christlikeness you see in people's character. Text a friend who's an especially good listener and let her know. Message someone on social media you know has been having a rough time and tell her you see God's strength in her, even if she doesn't feel it. When you choose to celebrate others, you show them the love of Christ and remind them how valued they are.

Even if you don't get the same encouragement back, you can move forward with confidence, knowing that God is most concerned with the status of your heart. He sees when you celebrate others and choose to take your eyes off yourself (and off your mirror). He sees how beautiful you are when you point out how wonderfully He's made someone else. He sees how gorgeous you look when you love others selflessly. And He is greatly pleased when you deliberately choose to fix your eyes and heart on what matters most—*Him*.[1]

READY TO GO DEEPER? Read Proverbs 4:23. How does this verse describe your heart? What does it mean to guard or be vigilant about your heart? Spend some time journaling about this and ask God to teach you more.

Pay It Forward

"Everyone who calls on the name of the Lord will be saved." How then will they call on him in whom they have not believed? And how are they to believe in him of whom they have never heard? And how are they to hear without someone preaching?

Romans 10:13–14

You never know where God's plan for your life will lead; it might be to a bus stop.

I (Bethany) had waited at this particular stop many times before, on the lookout for the bright yellow bus carrying the kids I nannied home from school. Maybe that's why I noticed her right away, the new girl waiting alongside the mamas and others I'd grown accustomed to seeing.

Never one to miss the chance to make a new friend, I introduced myself right away. Sara was not only new to my city, she was new to the US, having just arrived from Europe to be an au pair for a Texas family. After chatting for a few moments, Sara and I discovered the families we nannied for lived across the street from each other!

Sara and I hung out during playdates with the kids and met for coffee after work. It was fun enveloping my European friend into our big, crazy family. She even spent a couple holidays with us. Weeks sped into months and, all too soon, the time for Sara's return to Europe loomed close.

Though Sara and I had chatted about faith at various points, it became clear that she had little understanding of Jesus or the Bible. As she prepared to go back home, I couldn't shake this thought: *How can Sara know about Jesus unless someone tells her?* Deep breath. *Unless I tell her?*

Was I nervous to share what the Bible says with a friend who had very little understanding of it? Yes. But I knew that God's love for Sara was way bigger than my nervousness. I knew that He'd give me the strength and peace to communicate His gift of salvation to the friend I loved.

So I did. And it was amazing.

I bought a beautiful Bible for Sara and had her name printed on the cover. When she opened it, Sara told me it was the first Bible she had ever received. For a girl like me, raised in church with Bibles all over our house, that little fact gave me even more confidence: sharing God's truth with Sara was the most important thing in the world at that moment.

Our conversation was simple. I asked her to read John 3:16 and insert her own name in place of the words *the world*. In her beautifully accented voice, Sara read, "For God so loved *Sara*, that he gave his only Son, that if *Sara* believes in him, she should not perish but have eternal life." I showed Sara some passages I had marked and asked her if she'd be willing to read those too. Though I had hoped she'd choose to follow Jesus right then, that wasn't the way the story went. Actually, the story is still going!

Sara recently messaged me and told me, "I'm still reading the Bible you gave me." We may be an ocean apart, but our friendship goes on. I can continue to pray for her and encourage her. Who knows what God will do in her life and mine?

I know it can feel nerve-wracking to talk to someone about Jesus. I've left so many conversations wishing I'd been braver, wishing I'd taken more seriously what our verse of the day says. You and I have been given the most amazing gift of all—eternal life—and we have the chance to tell others about the incredible sacrifice Christ made for us.

Who is the Sara in your life right now? What brave step can you take to introduce her to Jesus? Let's be courageous together for the sake of the gospel!

READY TO GO DEEPER? Read the "Romans Road" (Rom. 3:23; 5:8; 6:23; and 10:9–10). Along with your personal testimony, these four verses can be used as a simple way to share God's gift of salvation. Here's another challenge for you: start memorizing one of these verses today!

Check Your Blind Spot

Let every person be quick to hear, slow to speak, slow to anger.

James 1:19

I (Kristen) love road trips, especially with my favorite people, going to my favorite places. Not too long ago, Zack and I piled into the car with three of my awesome siblings, adventured in Colorado, and after a fabulous time, headed back to Texas.

Little did I know that the conversation Zack started on the final stretch of our trip would become a defining moment in my spiritual growth.

The subject was controversial. The increase in heat had nothing to do with the car's thermostat or the season, and the final "score" was three against two, with Zack and I on opposite sides of the opinion fence. It was one of *those* car rides. We all love one another, though, so there was nothing ugly or mean; we just didn't agree. Zack and I hugged it out with the sibs before driving back to our place.

We had been home a few days when this car conversation came up again. My sweet husband gently pointed out some things I hadn't considered during the heat of my opinion campaign. As the man I love shared his thoughts with me, I realized I'd been blind to the way my critical words and intense opinions had come across.

According to the dictionary, a blind spot includes any "area or subject about which one is uninformed, prejudiced, or unappreciative."[1] Ugh! That totally hits home. I can all too often be uninformed about, prejudiced to, and unappreciative of others' thoughts and opinions. I hurt the people I love by being too slow to listen, too quick to speak, and too ready to criticize.

Whenever we're confronted in love with a spiritual blind spot, we have an important choice to make. I decided that day to humbly acknowledge to Zack that I had sinned. I had put my ideas, my thoughts, and my judgments ahead of everyone else's.

Please don't misunderstand me. I'm not saying that, as Christians, we should never disagree or that we should never feel strongly or even speak strongly about important things. Quite the opposite. But it's all about how and why we do what we do. Even when we're passionate about our opinions, we can still be quick to genuinely listen to the opinions of others (i.e., not hearing only to refute their ideas). We can be slow to barge in with our opinions and give more thought to our words. And we can certainly criticize less.

It's humbling to realize that we have blind spots. And we *all* do.

Are you willing to do something super brave today? Take a moment and ask God the Holy Spirit to reveal an area in which you have a blind spot. You can use Psalm 139:23–24 as a prayer:

> Search me, O God, and know my heart!
> Try me and know my thoughts!
> And see if there be any grievous way in me,
> and lead me in the way everlasting!

Listen quietly. Then write down what God brings to mind. Talk to someone you trust about what God is calling you to do.

I'm so proud of you for considering this challenge. May God lead you in the everlasting way of joy, love, and peace as you follow Him in this.

READY TO GO DEEPER? Read 2 Peter 1:5–10. According to this passage, what are the godly virtues that keep us from being nearsighted and blind? Which of these virtues would you like to work on first? Ask God for His help in this!

One of Our Faves

But the Lord GOD helps me;
therefore I have not been disgraced;
therefore I have set my face like a flint,
and I know that I shall not be put to shame.

Isaiah 50:7

Everyone's got a few favorite words. You know, the ones you use over and over. There's one we've used hundreds of times in GirlDefined Ministries.

Ready for it? Drum roll, please . . .

Intentional. And its derivatives: *intentionally* and *intentionality.* You get the picture.

For some, this might seem like an odd word to favor. But for us, it's huge. Being intentional is one of the main things that helps Christian girls enjoy the abundant life God died to give them (John 10:10). Why? Because delighting in God and growing spiritually don't just happen. The Christian life doesn't happen by accident. Maturity—and the outrageous joy that comes with it—boils down, in large part, to hundreds of intentional choices, made in the grace and power of the Holy Spirit.

Our husbands, Dāv (pronounced Dave) and Zack are great examples of intentionality. Zack intentionally spent three years finishing the education he needed, securing a job, and growing in his own faith before he pursued a dating relationship with me (Kristen). Before we got engaged, Dāv and I (Bethany) spent hours talking through over a hundred discussion questions aimed at helping us know each other's thoughts, opinions, hopes, and dreams. Both Zack and Dāv intentionally sought out our dad as a mentor and source of support. We're thankful for the intentionality of our godly men!

Intentionality wasn't something Zack and Dāv did for show or because they had to. As men who follow God, they were making deliberate choices. Our husbands reflect the truth of our verse for today—the person helped by God sets his face "like a flint."

For those of you who don't camp or regularly build your own fires, flint is a hard stone that is struck on a piece of steel to make fire. It's described, in short, as *unyielding*. When the Bible says that the people of God are helped by Him and unashamed, that they have faces set like flint, it describes those who cultivate intentional and unyielding godliness, a righteousness that doesn't change with trends or tastes.

We like the idea that, apart from being unyieldingly holy, an intentionally godly person can also spark a fire in the lives of others. You've probably heard the phrase "She's on fire for God." What if your life was so intentionally godly and so strong in Jesus that you helped spark His fire in others? That's exactly what we're getting after with the title of this book. That your life would *shine bright* for all to see and glorify your Father in heaven (Matt. 5:16).

There's one more thing we don't want you to miss about this passage. A lot of people today live with the crippling weight of shame. Shame is what we experience outside the redeeming grace of Christ. Maybe you've felt this.

One of the Bible's paths to freedom from shame is to intentionally choose to set our faces, like flint, on the One who covers all our guilt and sin. We can deliberately reject the lies culture tells us about our worth and dignity and believe the truth that sets us free instead (John 8:32): in Jesus Christ, we are accepted, beloved, honored, and treasured . . . *without exception.*

You can choose today which way you'll move—toward greater strength in Christ or away from it. We're intentionally moving toward strength, and we want you to join us.

READY TO GO DEEPER? Read Isaiah 49:1–3. What do you think it would look like for you to be a polished (aka sharpened) arrow for God's glory? How does this passage fit with our theme of intentionality?

Run in Such a Way

Therefore, since we are surrounded by so great a cloud of witnesses,
let us also lay aside every weight, and sin which clings so closely,
and let us run with endurance the race that is set before us, look-
ing to Jesus, the founder and perfecter of our faith, who for the joy
that was set before him endured the cross, despising the shame,
and is seated at the right hand of the throne of God.

Hebrews 12:1–2

When I (Bethany) signed up to run my first marathon, I pictured myself crossing the finish line with a huge smile on my face, the gorgeous Texas sun streaming down on me, and a crowd of family and friends cheering wildly.

What I didn't imagine was pouring rain and frigid cold creating knots in my burning calves. I didn't think I'd have to run for hours in silence because my sopping-wet earbuds wouldn't stay put. No one told me that going to the bathroom in the middle of the race could be such a nightmare, what with the cramping hands and soaking clothes. And that nifty belt that was supposed to hold my water bottles? Yeah, had to ditch that slippery sucker thanks to the rain too.

Honestly, though, all the craziness and pain faded into the distance when I got to that 26.2-mile marker. All those months of training paid off. I finished the race.

The verses from Hebrews that you read at the top of this devotional talk about running the race that is set before us, the race of life. This passage urges us to run the race with endurance by getting rid of extra weight (sin) so that we can cross the finish line with strength and joy.

One of the first (and coolest!) things about this passage is that it reminds us we don't have to run the race of life alone. We can look to Jesus while we go about our day. He's the only One who has been and will be with us throughout the entire race. He's the foundation of our faith and the One who perfects us.

We also see from these verses that a great "cloud of witnesses" surrounds us. This refers to all the brothers and sisters in Jesus—past, present, and future—who cheer us on. Just like my friends and family who braved pouring rain to help me make it through the marathon, your spiritual family can support you through the ups and downs of life's race. This is why Kristen and I always encourage those in the GirlDefined Sisterhood to be more than just members of a local church. We want you to be a vital part of your church community, to be friends with people who spur you on in Christ, and to be mentored by older women of faith. They are part of your "great cloud of witnesses"—the people who will be strong in prayer for you when you feel weak; the people who will know the good, the bad, and the ugly about you and love you just the same; the people who will remind you to fix your eyes on Jesus when you're tempted to focus instead on the rain in your life.

This passage also makes clear that we can't run well if we're holding on to anything but Christ. Sin tries to cling closely to us, but we have to lay aside its weight (sorta like me ditching the water-bottle belt). I had to let it go, no matter how useful or important it seemed at one point, no matter how much I had paid for or liked it. Friend, don't get weighed down by that sin clinging to you. You know the one I'm talking about. One of the best ways to lay aside sin is to confess it to God and to others. You don't have to do this alone! Go back and read the devotionals about confession and forgiveness (days 8 and 12) for help.

Even though today's verses are rich and have a lot of meaning, let me leave you with one more thing. These verses tell us to run with *endurance* and remind us that Jesus *endured* the cross. You probably caught the same root word—*endure*—in there. Honestly, it's a pretty intense word. It's a deliberate choice. But endurance is what the race of life calls for. One way I've heard the word *endure* described is to display strength through difficult situations, without giving way. Because Jesus endured the cross, we can endure everything through His power. In Him, you're stronger than you think. Whatever you might have to endure today, look to Jesus, remember you're not alone, and throw off every weight of sin. Kristen and I are running the race of faith next to you, and we're praying for you. You've got this, girl, 'cause He's got you.[1]

READY TO GO DEEPER? Journal about anything God is calling you to endure right now. What sin clings close to you? Ask God for help in laying aside its weight.

DAY 21

Something No One Needs to Be Taught

Do nothing from selfish ambition or conceit, but in humility count others more significant than yourselves. Let each of you look not only to his own interests, but also to the interests of others.

Philippians 2:3–4

While out shopping a while ago, I (Kristen) came across two girls chatting near some accessory displays. I couldn't hear what they were saying, but it was obvious they were friends. As I got nearer, one girl started to tell the other something that looked really important to her. She went on for a bit, then paused. I watched this girl's face fall; she had been talking into a void. Her friend had abandoned the story and was picking up a cute purse a couple tables away.

Have you ever felt less important to someone than a purse? Or a text? Or a "like"? I have. It hurts, doesn't it? I hate thinking that I've made other people feel that way sometimes.

Growing up, we all had to be taught the "magic words"— please and thank you. We all had to learn to eat with table manners. But no one had to teach us to put ourselves first. That came without practice. *My*, *mine*, and *no* are three words every toddler knows how to wield like weapons. We never needed to be taught selfishness because it's in every single one of us.

Yuck. That truth is no fun. But, if you ask me, it's becoming more apparent every day. It's now more likely that people will livestream someone in a dangerous situation than jump in to help them. It's more often than not that people treat each other as less significant than the phones in their pockets. Do you know what I mean?

As Christians, we're called to something radically different. The verses at the top of this page invite us to reject the selfishness inside and deliberately choose to think of others. Notice something crucial: these verses don't say Christians should never take their own needs into consideration. On the contrary! The Bible says don't look out *only* for yourself.

Selfishness comes in many forms. For some people it's a look-out-for numero-uno, get-out-of-my-way-so-I-can-rule-the-world attitude. For others it shows up as an I'm-the-star-and-y'all-are-just-my-supporting-cast mentality. But these are the obvious kinds of selfishness.

Maybe you know some people who are "self-reflectors"? When you talk to them, everything goes back to their life, their opinions, their plans. Self-reflectors never ask you a question because they're only thinking about how you fit into *their* life.

At times a person's insecurity can also be an expression of selfishness. When a girl is so worried about what other people think that she can't spare a thought for the needs of others, self-focus is a bigger threat to her than insecurity.

Jesus gave us the perfect example for how to overcome selfishness. And I'll give you a hint: the answer isn't to obsess about how much you think about yourself. The answer is to turn out-ward rather than inward. The answer is to choose love. In John 13:34–35, Jesus tells us that others will know we are His because of our love for one another.

So, let's be girls who look out for others, not just ourselves, girls who won't abandon a friend for a cute purse (or a cuter boy) or a snap-worthy photo. Let's be girls who are so secure in God's love that we can love others without worrying about ourselves all the time. Let's be girls who ask questions and stay interested in what our friends have to say. Let's fight the rise of selfishness with greater love. You with me?

READY TO GO DEEPER? Read all of Philippians 2. What example does Jesus set for us? How does this chapter invite you to live with greater love for others?

Your Outfit of the Day

Put on then, as God's chosen ones, holy and beloved, compassionate hearts, kindness, humility, meekness, and patience.

Colossians 3:12

If you've watched any of our online videos, it's probably apparent that we enjoy cute clothes, makeup, an aesthetically pleasing set design, chic home decor . . . basically all things pretty. We totally enjoy dressing up and trying out new styles (although a good topknot and sweatpants are weekly favorites too). Having fun with fashion and enjoying beauty are great aspects of our lives as women, but we know there are more important things for us to put on than makeup and a cute outfit.

In our verse for today, God calls us to put on certain character qualities: compassion, kindness, humility, meekness, and patience. The Greek words that we translate in English as "put on" literally mean to "invest with clothing." In other words, because we're God's chosen ones, holy and beloved, we should clothe ourselves with beautiful hearts, hearts full of the traits He listed.

Let's start with the word *compassion*, since that's where God starts the list in Colossians 3:12. On the simplest level, the word *compassion* means "shared emotion." You feel what someone else feels. Dictionary.com actually gives an excellent definition for compassion: "A feeling of deep sympathy and sorrow for another who is stricken by misfortune, accompanied by a strong desire to alleviate the suffering."[1]

In a world where people are rapidly losing their ability to feel one another's pain or go beyond themselves to end someone else's suffering, being clothed with a compassionate heart stands out, pointing people to Jesus in a powerful way. In fact, more than any other word, *compassionate* is used in the Bible to describe Jesus's heart and actions![2] Jesus looked at the hurting and lost, the brokenhearted and afraid and felt compassion for them. Can you see why God would call us to put on a compassionate heart? He knows we tend to get wrapped up in our own troubles. Looking out for others and developing a compassionate heart are truly countercultural and Christlike.

God also calls us to put on kindness. At first you might think, *Well, isn't that a lot like compassion?* Kindness actually pairs with compassion. Compassion sees and hurts; kindness acts. Kindness jumps in and shows grace, even to the undeserving. Biblical kindness isn't something we can muster up, and it certainly isn't random. Kindness is a deliberate act of love. How often would you say you intentionally "put on" kindness? If you're anything like us, you probably could grow in this area, especially when someone's been unkind to you.

We want to say much more, but for today, look for ways you can start "putting on" compassion and kindness. Pray that God would open your eyes to ways you're not currently clothing yourself with these godly traits. And then come back tomorrow to learn about three more pieces of your godly wardrobe.

READY TO GO DEEPER? Read Galatians 5:22. How does this list fit with what you read today? According to Galatians 5:22, who is the source of godly character? Ask the Holy Spirit to help you put on the right spiritual wardrobe today.

Your Outfit of the Day #2

*Put on then, as God's chosen ones, holy and beloved,
compassionate hearts, kindness, humility, meekness, and
patience.*

Colossians 3:12

Before we dive in to unveiling part 2 of the most beautiful wardrobe we can develop, we don't want you to miss what Colossians 3:12 reminds us about ourselves. Girl, you are chosen, holy, and beloved in Jesus. Don't ever forget it! There may be days you'll feel like no one wants you, days you feel dirty and ashamed, days you can't feel God's love. Our feelings and emotions lie to us sometimes. Who you are—the truth about who you are in Christ—is clear: you are accepted, set apart, and passionately loved. Always! Until the very end.

And it's because of our confidence in being chosen, holy, and beloved that we can ditch the worldly wardrobe of self, self, and more self. Instead, we can put on humility and meekness. Okay, but what on earth does it mean to put on humility and meekness? These aren't words people use every day.

Looking back on how Jesus lived here on earth helps us understand the perfect definition of *humility*. The Bible tells us that Christ did not come to be served, but to serve (Matt. 20:28).

Jesus thought of others before Himself (read Philippians 2 for a great explanation of this!). It doesn't say Jesus never thought about Himself or that He thought badly about Himself. In a sense, humility isn't about thinking less of yourself but rather choosing to think of yourself less.

Meekness, too, is often misunderstood as a nice way of saying *weakness*. This is not what the Bible teaches. The word *meek* means great strength under perfect control. When Jesus walked on earth, He had all the power that created the world within Him, but He knew how to use that power in the right ways, at the right times. You've probably come across people who *don't* keep their power under control. They're sometimes difficult to be around. As a girl defined by God, you have been given an infinite connection to power—the Holy Spirit lives within you! When you choose to harness the power you've got with self-control, you show the world that it's possible to be strong and humble at the same time. According to God, that's *real* girl power.

To round out the list, God urges us to put on patience. Yes, this one is tough. You've probably figured out that the two of us both have full-throttle personalities. We talk fast, think fast, and live high-octane lives. We have to intentionally put on patience; it doesn't happen by accident. In fact, the opposite is usually true. In default mode, we're *not* the most patient women in the world. Maybe you can relate? I think that's why God gave us this list and why patience is on there; He knows that we'll have to choose, over and over again, to put on patience. *Patient* perfectly describes God's love toward us: He doesn't give way to anger but restrains His wrath, giving us grace and mercy instead. Since so much has been given to us, can't we learn patience too?

So, today, before you put on your mascara or your favorite shirt, put on compassion, kindness, humility, meekness, and patience.

READY TO GO DEEPER? Which of these character traits is the hardest for you to put on? Journal about it. Consider printing Colossians 3:12 and taping it to your mirror so you can memorize this powerful list.

DAY 24
The Gift No One Wants

So we do not lose heart. Though our outer self is wasting away, our inner self is being renewed day by day. For this light momentary affliction is preparing for us an eternal weight of glory beyond all comparison, as we look not to the things that are seen but to the things that are unseen. For the things that are seen are transient, but the things that are unseen are eternal.

2 Corinthians 4:16–18

If you were to meet me (Bethany) for the first time, there would be a few things immediately apparent to you. I'm tall, like *really* tall (6'1"). I'm super outgoing. And I love life. What you probably wouldn't guess, though, after meeting me for the first time is that I battle chronic pain.

Maybe it's because I'm a cheerful person. Maybe it's because I do a lot and have high energy. I'm not totally certain why it surprises people to find out that I've battled debilitating migraine headaches for years, but I've lost more days and seen more plans crash and burn while lying in bed, trying to keep light and sound to an absolute minimum, than I could ever count. Not gonna lie—fighting migraines is miserable.

Like most people, I actively try to avoid pain. I'd gladly eradicate the migraines from my life if given the choice. But I've also learned a lot through my pain. I'm not sure I can completely understand it yet, but I've started to see that pain can draw me closer to God and help me know Him in deeper ways. In that way it's a gift. A really hard gift.

I remember one day in particular when I was exiled to my bed, fighting waves of nausea, and God brought to mind something I'd heard in a sermon. Like a diamond, which must endure extreme heat, pressure, cutting, and polishing to achieve sparkling brilliance, our character must endure intense difficulty to shine brightly. I can view pain either as an enemy to be defeated at all costs or as part of the pressure and polishing that makes me more beautiful for Jesus. The prayers I've prayed during my many hours in bed, the comfort God has given me, the gratitude for each day of health I do have are priceless gifts that have changed me . . . for the better. I shine more brightly because of my struggle, and you can too.

You're going to face pain in your life. I know . . . super upbeat message, right?

But you already know it's true. Sometimes your body will hurt. Other times it will be your heart. As you grow in Christ, there may be times your soul aches for someone you love who doesn't know Jesus or someone you care about who's making terrible decisions. What will you do with the pain in your life?

If you follow the world's path, you'll try to get rid of the pain, numbing it by abusing drugs or alcohol, binge watching TV shows, or endlessly scrolling social media. But if you receive the gift pain offers—the gift of closeness with God—you'll find that, while you can't end pain, it doesn't have to end you.

The verses you read at the beginning of today's devotional remind us that, even when we feel like everything is falling apart,

God is still at work. He's preparing for us (and us for) an eternal glory suited to the precious treasure you're becoming through His refining process. Girl, fix your eyes with me on what really lasts!

No matter what kind of pain you're facing today or will face tomorrow, you can move forward with confidence, knowing that—on the inside, where things count—you're being made new by God. Instead of looking at your pain, turn your eyes to Jesus. He promises that, one day, "He will wipe away every tear from their eyes, and death shall be no more, neither shall there be mourning, nor crying, nor pain anymore, for the former things have passed away" (Rev. 21:4). Sister, that's a promise worth living for, even when life hurts.[1]

READY TO GO DEEPER? Is it easy or difficult for you to imagine pain could be a gift? Talk to God about it. Read Psalm 34. What does God say about the brokenhearted? How do you respond to this promise?

The Secret to Better Friendships

Jesus turned and saw them following and said to them, "What are you seeking?"

John 1:38

If you met our younger sister Ellissa today, you would never guess how shy and reserved she once was. Ellissa is so full of life, love, and laughter, it's crazy that just a few years ago, the same girl who travels to China to love on orphaned children tried to hide in the sanctuary rather than hang out with people during youth group. God has done a powerful work in Ellissa's heart, making her a young woman who others feel comfortable and confident around. One of the major ways Jesus did this was through teaching her the power and purpose behind asking good questions.

Ellissa and I (Kristen) practiced asking good questions during one of our mentoring coffee dates. I knew that this would make her a better conversationalist, which—in turn—would make her a better friend. In his classic book *How to Win Friends and Influence People*, Dale Carnegie describes it well: "You can make more friends in two months by becoming interested in other people than you can in two years by trying to get other people interested in you.... If we merely try to impress people and get people interested in us, we will never have many true, sincere friends. Friends, real friends, are not made that way."[1] Why? Because people want to know that you care about them, that you want to know them.

Did you ever imagine that asking good questions would be the secret to better friendships? It is! Jesus modeled this, showing us again and again how questions open people's hearts. In the four Gospels, Jesus asks over two hundred questions. If you read through Matthew, Mark, Luke, and John, it's clear that Jesus was the master question asker.

Jesus asked questions to get people thinking, to reveal their true intentions, to get closer to them. If you're looking to build lasting, quality friendships—friendships that go beyond likes and shared selfies—ask the kinds of get-closer-to-people questions that Jesus asked.

In John 1, two disciples were intrigued by what their teacher, John the Baptist, said about Jesus (see vv. 15–36). They immediately left John and began to follow Jesus. I'm not sure what I would have expected Jesus to say to two of His first disciples, but "What are you seeking?" probably wouldn't have topped my list. Wasn't it obvious what they sought? You know . . . the Savior. The Rescuer who John the Baptist declared Jesus to be.

Just as He often does, Jesus blows our expectations out of the water. He asked two of His first disciples a question that helped them know their own hearts better. We can do this too. Not that I'm saying when you make a new friend you should start out with "What do you want from me?" Awkward!

Instead, we can ask questions to show people we really care about them and they can be known and safe with us. If you want to be a better friend and have better friendships, learn to ask good questions. To get started with this, check out the archives on our website, www.GirlDefined.com. Search "How the Art of Conversation Has Transformed My Life" by our sweet friend and guest blogger Elizabeth.[2] You can also access videos we've done, like "How to Build Friendships."[3] And you can meet Ellissa and hear more of her story by searching "My Story of Overcoming Social Fear and Worry."[4] We'll see you over at the website soon!

READY TO GO DEEPER? Read John 15:5. What does Jesus call us to in this verse? How does that make you feel? How does it change your friendships to know that Jesus calls you His friend?

Scorched or Strong?

*And the L*ORD *will guide you continually*
and satisfy your desire in scorched places
and make your bones strong;
and you shall be like a watered garden,
like a spring of water,
whose waters do not fail.

Isaiah 58:11

Confession time: I (Kristen) have the opposite of a green thumb. What would that be . . . a red thumb? It's an odd but pretty accurate picture of how well I take care of plants. Pity the poor living greenery that comes through my door or onto my porch. I just can't seem to keep things alive.

Though I'd like to blame all my disastrous gardening on external forces, that just wouldn't be true. Yes, some plants are harder to keep than others, but when it comes down to it, there's one consistent thing I struggle to do: water my plants. And without water? Yeah. You know where things go from there.

After a summer of watching the beautiful potted flowers I had brought home die a slow, crackly, brownish death (LOL—that sounds so dramatic), Bethany told me she low-key judged me for not making it a priority to water the plants. But then we both realized that the undernourished plants perishing on my front step gave us a picture of what happens spiritually when we forget to get daily nourishment from time alone with God.

Take a sec to reread the verse at the top of this page.

If you ask me, Isaiah 58:11 is a *wow!* kind of verse. The picture that we will be guided, satisfied, strong—like a garden whose waters never fail—is breathtakingly beautiful. What's really crazy? We don't even have to do the watering! We just have to show up in God's presence; His living water does it all. His Word nourishes us. Prayer strengthens us. Listening enables us to live out His promises. And worship goes down into our very bones, strengthening us even when we're in "scorched places."

Jesus affirmed this to an outsider, a woman most religious people wouldn't have bothered to notice, let alone talk to (see John 4). Standing at the well from which the woman came to draw water, Jesus declared, "Everyone who drinks of this water will be thirsty again, but whoever drinks of the water that I will give him will never be thirsty again. The water that I will give him will become in him a spring of water welling up to eternal life" (John 4:13–14).

Don't let your life wither when you know the source of living water. Don't let your strength fade away because you forget to spend time with God. Don't let yourself become dry and brittle because you've decided you don't need to be alone with God. Instead, let God's Word fill you to the point that you're overflowing and thriving![1]

READY TO GO DEEPER? Read Isaiah 43:15–21. What does verse 19 say? How does this relate to what you read today? Are you feeling dry or well watered today? Journal about it, asking God to help you grow through His Word.

DAY 27

I Don't Get It

Jesus answered him, "What I am doing you do not understand now, but afterward you will understand."

John 13:7

Most of us didn't realize how much would be lost when COVID-19 became widespread throughout the world in 2020. It seemed like everyone lost something as a result of the coronavirus pandemic. Everyone lost time with friends. Everyone knew someone who got sick. Some lost jobs; others lost loved ones. Weddings were canceled. Hospitals admitted no visitors. Loneliness skyrocketed. In an instant, our world changed.

It was super hard for many people to understand why God would allow such an awful pandemic to start. It was difficult to figure out what God was doing. Loss hurts. It was heartbreaking to see so many people in pain—whether physical sickness, financial struggle, relationship strains, or sadness about losing things that had been planned and anticipated.

John 13:7 offers comfort in our confusion. Bottom line, there are times when we just don't understand why God is doing what He's doing. We may not completely comprehend it until we're safely on the other side, surrounded by His love and peace forever.

God fully engages with our questions and confusion. He can handle our anger and frustration (read the books of Psalms and Job if you doubt this). He understands that we're humans who often feel desperate and afraid. He doesn't scold us for feeling bummed to miss out on our sports season, graduation, job, or time with friends. He also knows what it's like to be human! He lived here. Isaiah 53:3 says He was "a man of sorrows and acquainted with grief."

In John 11, Jesus stood at the grave of one of His best friends. He cried there. He knows what it's like to lose someone. He fully understands the anguish that weighs on people who have lost loved ones.

When we just don't get it, when we're confused and afraid, we can remember that Jesus is with us. Even though we don't always understand what He's up to, there *will* be a day when all of it will make sense. His promises remain true. Reread our verse for today: "Afterward you will understand."

Jesus said this to His disciples right before He was arrested and crucified. Talk about not getting it! The disciples were totally baffled by this. They believed He would deliver them from their enemies (the Romans) and set up a kingdom of peace. Jesus's death *did* accomplish those things. The disciples just didn't understand how at that moment. Afterward they did. They saw that Jesus defeated the true enemies, the final enemies: sin and death. They saw that the kingdom He set up was an everlasting kingdom of peace, not an earthly one bound by space, time, and matter. They didn't get it in the moment, but truth made a way into their hearts. The disciples saw, and we can see—if we look with the eyes of faith.

We're not sure where this devotional finds you today. You may see God working through the difficult circumstances in your life. You may feel confused and disappointed. Grief may haunt you. Wherever you're at, His promise is true: there will be a day when you will understand, a day when He will make all things new. Hang on, sister; that day is coming.

READY TO GO DEEPER? Read Psalm 57:1. What does the psalmist say God will do when trouble comes? Journal a prayer, talking to God about your experience during the most recent trial in your life.

Friends Who Pick You Up

Two are better than one, because they have a good reward
for their toil. For if they fall, one will lift up his fellow.
But woe to him who is alone when he falls and has not
another to lift him up!

Ecclesiastes 4:9–10

Some people have a hard time remembering their most embarrassing moments. I (Bethany) don't have that particular struggle. Girl, I've got stories to tell. Allow me to regale you with one of my tales.

Like many I-want-to-sink-into-the-floor stories, this one started with me feeling pretty great about myself. My sophomore year in high school, my basketball team had just won a huge tournament, and I was waiting with my friends for the trophy presentation. As the announcer called our team to the stage, I started down a big flight of stairs. In my excitement (and pride), I decided to slide down the rest on the railing. Only problem? I lost my balance, flipped over backward, ended up on my head, and launched everything I had been carrying across the gym floor. Making matters even worse? A bunch of guys were right behind me, watching the entire horrible spectacle unfold. Yeah.

So, what's the moral of this story? That pride goes before destruction and a haughty spirit before a fall, like Proverbs 16:18 promises? Yes, that's true. And I was definitely puffed up with some pride that day.

But this devotional is about something else. It's about what happened *after* one of the most embarrassing moments of my teenage life. In a split second, my basketball team surrounded me, helping me up off the floor and scooping up my scattered things. Instead of laughing at me, worrying about what the guys behind us thought, or—in today's day and age—recording my fall for social media, my friends picked me up ... literally! I was so grateful that those girls weren't just on my team but on my side.

That day, I learned that who you surround yourself with makes a huge difference! Do the girls you hang with right now pick each other up or tear each other down? What would your friends do if something like my epic fall happened to you? If you're friends mostly with "takers," or with people who rip one another apart when someone walks out of the room, it's time to make a change. You don't have to stay in a toxic friend group just because you've always been friends or you don't think you have anyone else. God will bring the right kind of friends if you trust Him and choose wisely who to invest your time and energy in befriending. And keep in mind that you might have to let go of something (a friend group, a particular friend, or even a boyfriend) before God can give you what's best.

At the same time, be the kind of friend you would like to have. In Luke 6:31, Jesus tells us to treat others the way we want to be treated. If you want to have the right kind of friends—friends who will pick you up, no matter what—be that kind of friend to others. You can start today.[1]

READY TO GO DEEPER? Read Luke 6:27–36. What does this passage teach? Is this easy or difficult for you to do? Journal about it, talking to God about anyone you may feel tempted to leave out of this command.

DAY 29

The Secret to Inner Peace

I have learned in whatever situation I am to be content. I know how to be brought low, and I know how to abound. In any and every circumstance, I have learned the secret of facing plenty and hunger, abundance and need. I can do all things through him who strengthens me.

Philippians 4:11–13

I (Kristen) will never, ever forget when I learned the truth of the oft-quoted saying "You always want what you can't have . . ."

Can you finish that statement? I imagine you can, or at least you'll recognize it when I fill in the blank: "and then when you get it, you don't want it anymore."

I've always admired full, luscious locks. My hair is on the thinner side, and it had always bugged me prior to this experience. When I complimented a girl on her gorgeous do and she confided in me that she had hair extensions, let's just say my interest was piqued. I got the details and made an appointment not too long afterward.

When the stylist was done braiding the extensions (and we're talkin' real, beautiful hair) at the very base of my scalp, near my neck, I was shocked at how natural it looked. I felt like a million bucks! I relished my new commercial-worthy hair for the next few weeks.

And then . . .

Fingering through my hair after a shower one day, I noticed that the extensions had knotted a bit. I tried to undo them, to no avail. My mom and sister also came to help. We scoured the Internet for tips, trying everything to get out the knots. Nothing worked. After several hours, I finally surrendered; mom would have to unbraid the extensions. I was about to lose my gorgeous, full hairdo.

I wish I could say that was the end of it, but things went from bad to worse. Even after all her efforts to undo what I'd paid to have braided (and what I had prided myself on), my mom had to cut out a huge section of my hair. I lost not only the extensions but also about a third of my natural hair in one awful moment.

Sister, I know that it's tough to stay content in an age that tells us, "If you don't like something about yourself, change it!" Beyond applying makeup, transforming wardrobes, getting waxed, threaded, and weaved, the number of girls under twenty-five who opt for plastic surgery has skyrocketed.

As a girl, being content with your physical appearance is hard enough. Add to that the issue of being content with the money you have (or don't), the relationships you have (or don't), and the opportunities you may (or may not) get, and it's a perfect storm raging against what God teaches us: "Godliness with contentment is great gain" (1 Tim. 6:6).

Contentment doesn't come naturally to us. Since Eve in the garden, girls have always wanted what they don't have. But there's a powerful truth tucked away in today's verses. Paul says he *learned* contentment. It didn't just happen, but it wasn't impossible either. Why? Because Paul also learned he could "do all things through him who strengthens [him]" (Phil. 4:13).

People often use this verse in a sort of pump-you-up, you-can-be-anything-you-want-to-be way. But the context of this verse is bigger than that. Philippians 4 teaches us that—no matter what—we can learn to be at peace. Whether we have a lot or a little, we can learn contentment. And to learn, we have to pay attention and study.

So, let me ask you, which are you studying today: contentment or dissatisfaction? I learned the hard way that contentment is great gain, but you don't have to learn the hard way. Choose contentment, and you'll experience His strength in all things. That's His promise, not mine. And for a deeper study on the topics of beauty and identity, check out our book *Girl Defined: God's Radical Design for Beauty, Femininity, and Identity*.

READY TO GO DEEPER? Read Hebrews 13:5. Why does this passage tell us to be content? If God will never leave us or forsake us, when will we be "without"? Spend some time surrendering to God the things you've felt discontent about. Ask Him to help you learn contentment.

Do the Next Right Thing

She did what she could.

Mark 14:8[1]

Once upon a time, Disney really got it right. As a young princess faces the loss of everything she holds most dear, she bravely stands and sings. And while Disney movies aren't usually a reliable source for biblical truth or wisdom, the song "Do the Next Right Thing" resonates with a powerful truth Jesus taught. Sometimes you simply need to do what you can. And that's enough.

Here's the setting for Mark 14. A couple days before the biggest festival of the Jewish year, Passover, Jesus traveled to a small town outside Jerusalem. He was invited to dine at the house of a man who the Bible calls "Simon the Leper." We can pick up the story in verse 3, when "a woman came with an alabaster jar of very expensive perfume, made of pure nard. She broke the jar and poured the perfume on his head. Some of those present were saying indignantly to one another, 'Why this waste of perfume? It could have been sold for more than a year's wages and the money given to the poor.' And they rebuked her harshly" (Mark 14:3–5).

The self-righteous people at Simon's dinner party considered what this woman did foolish at best, definitely misguided, probably sinful. Jesus saw things differently. "'Leave her alone,' said

Jesus. 'Why are you bothering her? She has done a beautiful thing to me. The poor you will always have with you, and you can help them any time you want. But you will not always have me. *She did what she could.* She poured perfume on my body beforehand to prepare for my burial. Truly I tell you, wherever the gospel is preached throughout the world, what she has done will also be told, in memory of her'" (Mark 14:6–9, emphasis added).

In the ancient world, women could do very little. They were restricted, looked down on, and mistreated in ways we—girls raised in a much freer world—can't even fathom. We're certainly not saying things are perfect for women in every part of today's world (far from it!), but during Jesus's time, women had very few opportunities and a horde of opponents.

Jesus, however, always treated women—including the woman who blessed him at Simon's party—with dignity, respect, and love. He constantly defied the norms for a man in the ancient world, let alone a respected religious teacher, by caring for, conversing with, and cherishing women.

When He turned the situation in Mark on its head by approving of this woman and her courageous act of love, Jesus observed that "she did what she could." She did the next right thing, and it was beautiful to Jesus.

What is the "next right thing" God is asking you to do today? You can't conquer racism in one day, but maybe you can stand up to the bullies at your school or on your social media feed. You may not be able to fix greed on a global scale, but can you say no to consumerism and the lie of "more" by *not* buying into the latest fad? Maybe God wants you to simply turn off the TV or shut off your phone for a time so that you can focus more on the people right next to you. Do the next right thing, no matter how small. And then do the next right thing after that. The two of us are doing that with you!

READY TO GO DEEPER? Read Matthew 25:23. With what words does Jesus tell us He will welcome His beloved children home? Journal about what it would look like for you to live a life "well done."

DAY 31
Therefore, I Have Hope

My soul is downcast within me.
Yet this I call to mind
   and therefore I have hope:
Because of the LORD's great love we are not consumed,
   for his compassions never fail.
They are new every morning;
   great is your faithfulness.

                                  Lamentations 3:20–23¹

It was heartache like I (Kristen) had never experienced. My first miscarriage stole the very breath within me; pain I still can't fully explain descended on me. And then there was the second baby lost six months later. And then the third. God, why did You take three babies Zack and I desperately wanted home to heaven before we could kiss their sweet little heads and tell them how much they were loved? I understood—more than I ever had—the biblical word *downcast*. I really did feel cast down, pressed in on every side with grief and confusion.

Motherhood may be a long way off for some of you, or you may have endured a miscarriage already. Either way, you probably know exactly what it's like to feel hopeless. And it doesn't have to be because of something similar to what Zack and I have suffered. Hopelessness can come in many forms—fears about the future, heartache from broken relationships, the death of a dream you held dear.

What got me through the dark days after each of my losses? God's love. His presence. And His life-giving Word.

The verses I chose for today's devotional, from a book of the Bible lots of people haven't even heard of, have strengthened me like nothing else during those agonizing times.

Notice that the prophet Jeremiah, who wrote Lamentations, doesn't deny his hurt. The Bible invites us to be brutally honest about our suffering. He acknowledges that his soul aches. In fact, the first twenty verses of Lamentations 3 describe Jeremiah's pain in heartbreaking detail.

And then the tide turns.

"Yet this I call to mind and therefore I have hope . . ."

Even though pain has gripped me, even throughout this very misery, what I choose can give me hope. What you choose can give you hope too.

What did Jeremiah call to mind? What have I been calling to mind for the many years of my infertility and recurrent miscarriages? God's unfailing love. His compassion that never ends. The mercy He pours out anew every single morning. And *therefore I have hope.*

Once upon a time, I heard that when you see the word *therefore* in Scripture, ask what it's there for. It's a little corny, I know, but actually super helpful. So, what's the *therefore* in Lamentations 3 there for? To show us where to find hope!

We can't look for hope in our circumstances changing. I hate this reality, but some things on earth never change. We can't look for hope within, because neither you nor I can conjure up enough positive energy to hope through the hardest things in life.

We can discover and hold on to hope only in the One who will never change, never walk out, never lose. In His love, in His care, in His promises, I have hope. You can too.

Life hurts sometimes. You don't have to pretend it doesn't. You can also have hope. I'm so grateful for God's love, compassion, and mercy. Lean into them with me, my sister and friend.

READY TO GO DEEPER? Read John 14:27 and 16:33. Take some time to journal about the things that Jesus promises in these two verses.

A Game Changer

What you have learned and received and heard and seen in me—practice these things, and the God of peace will be with you.

Philippians 4:9

We spend a lot of time practicing something we learned years ago because it changes lives: mentoring. Godly older women have invested so much time in us, and it's truly been transformational. As a result, we meet one-on-one for coffee dates with girls younger than us (including our sisters!). GirlDefined offers an online mentorship course for girls around the world, we blog and vlog about mentoring, and we offer breakout sessions at our yearly conference focused on the importance of mentoring. Is all of this a bit overboard, you might wonder? No way! We've lived the reality that mentoring really does make a difference.

The Bible describes mentorship in several key ways. The book of Proverbs details the importance of gaining wisdom and seeking counsel. Titus 2 outlines specific topics and relationships. And we see from Philippians 4:9 that putting into practice what you hear, receive, and learn from a mentor can lead to a greater experience of God's peace. I don't know any girl who doesn't want greater peace in her life! So, let's look at how mentoring works.

Like most things in the Christian walk, mentorship begins with prayer. Ask God to bring to mind a godly woman, preferably older than you, to whom you can talk about life and faith. You may already have a youth leader at church or a Bible study leader on your college campus in mind. Perhaps God will guide you to connect with someone new. Though I (Kristen) had to overcome a few nerves to ask someone to mentor me, I'm so grateful God nudged me in that direction. It's made such a difference in my life! When I (Bethany) started dating Dāv, I asked my mentor a zillion questions and got specific, godly help. I can't tell you how awesome that was.

After you've prayed about it, gotten the nerve to ask someone to mentor you, and she's said yes, you can start meeting together. You may meet frequently or less often. You may meet in person or digitally. You may read through a book of the Bible or a Christian book together. You'll definitely talk about life—the great things and the struggles—and pray together. Regardless of how you do the things you do, the goal of godly mentoring is to lead you closer to Jesus.

Did you catch from today's verse that to make mentoring work, you need to commit to one important thing? You've got to *practice* what you hear, receive, and learn from your mentor. It doesn't help much, even if you're meeting every single week, to listen and not do anything your mentor suggests. If she encourages you to do something wise, put it into practice!

Last thing: don't be discouraged if it takes a while to find a mentor. If you're praying and trusting God, He'll guide you to a mentor who is just right for you. And girl, that's gonna be awesome![1]

READY TO GO DEEPER? Read Titus 2:3–5. What are some of the things this passage says an older woman can teach you right now? What things (like tips for raising kids) might you learn from a mentor later? Spend some time today praying for a mentor.

I Surrender

Not my will, but yours, be done.

Luke 22:42

At seventeen years old, at twenty, at twenty-four—I (Bethany) remember so clearly three times God asked me to surrender.

Basketball had been my passion for years. When I wasn't playing or practicing, I was talking or thinking, even dreaming, about basketball. Turning seventeen and getting closer to high school graduation meant getting scouted by colleges and being offered some amazing scholarships—to Division 1 teams. It felt incredible! This was everything I'd been working toward and hoping for. Or was it?

The more I prayed about accepting the offers, the less peace I felt. I sought counsel from godly family and friends. I prayed hard. I thought about every possibility. I prayed more. And it finally became clear: God was inviting me to surrender this dream. I *did* believe He had a better plan for me, but that didn't make it easy to trust. Turning down those scholarships felt like a big deal, but I chose to put my faith in God more than in a college opportunity.

Several years later, Kristen and I considered attending Bible school together. We applied and got accepted. It seemed like the right thing to do. All the planning and prep went well. Then, in some pretty crazy ways, God moved both of us in a different direction. I knew God had something else for me, but—again—I didn't know exactly what that was. It was hard to surrender this dream, too, but I believed God would make His will clear.

Fast-forward a few more years, and I was dating a guy I really liked. Like really, really liked. I didn't want to surrender this relationship to God, even though I could see some major red flags. Girl, I cried so many nights. I *did not* want to give this relationship up to the Lord. Jesus was so gentle with me. It was hard, but I let go of this guy. I told God, "Not my will, but yours, be done." I share more about this in *Love Defined: Discovering God's Vision for Lasting Love and Satisfying Relationships*.

Surrender can be super tough. It's not even a word that gets much respect. The world makes it seem like surrendering equals being a coward, living in defeat, shrinking into a smaller life. God says the opposite. Surrendering to Jesus requires a lot of strength; it leads to victory and a greater life in Him.

When I hold on to my plans and dreams too tightly, it's like I'm clenching my fists. I'm gripping the things that feel good and safe. But holding on so tightly to one thing (or multiple things) means I can't receive what Jesus wants to give me—something that will be far better if I can bravely trust Him. Surrender means opening my hands, telling God that I believe His will is best, and lifting my open hands to Him. Open, uplifted hands are a sign not only that I'm ready to receive what He has for me but also that I worship Him above all my dreams and desires.

Saying "Not my will, but yours, be done" may feel risky to you. That's okay. Talk to God about it. Ask Him to help you trust

Him more. Pray for His help in seeing His good plan for your life. Sister, surrendering to God may just be the bravest and the best thing you and I ever do.

READY TO GO DEEPER? Read Jeremiah 29:11–13. How does it make you feel to know that you will find the Lord if you seek Him?

Your Most Valuable Resource

Teach us to number our days
that we may get a heart of wisdom.
Psalm 90:12

Isn't it weird how some days fly by and other days just *drag*? Typically, fun times are gone before you know it, but days when you have an afternoon exam or a doctor's appointment? Why do they crawl by so miserably?

Time can be really odd, right? We can kill time, save time, lose time. We all spend time too. Philosophers may tell us, "Time is the most valuable thing [anyone] can spend,"[1] but no one can control it. Time flows on and on, never stopping to consider what we want, hope for, or need.

Have you ever considered this? God created time. He created time just like He created the heavens and the earth, pigs and pelicans, you and me. That's a wild thought, isn't it? And wouldn't it make sense, if God created time, that He might have a thing or two to tell us about it?

He does.

In fact, the Bible speaks about time pretty often. If you ask us, that's because what we invest our time in shapes our entire lives. According to the Bible, the philosophers are on point: time is the most valuable thing we can spend.

That's why Psalm 90:12 is an important verse. It's a prayer, written by Moses, the man God used to bring His people out of slavery in Egypt. Moses had over a century to think about time (he lived to be 120), so when he asks God, "Teach us to number our days that we may get a heart of wisdom," we'd do well to pay attention.

What does it mean to "number our days" though? God's not telling us to count the number of our days, like life is one long math lesson. He's also not encouraging us to calculate the number of days we'll live. Instead, He's urging us to live in the present day as if it's our very last. Turns out, the "Live now" and "Today is all you've got" messages you may have heard actually have biblical origins.

God invites us, through Psalm 90 and other passages, to seriously consider how short life can be. Many of us started thinking about this more after the coronavirus pandemic began. Others of you who go to school may think of this every time another active shooter attack happens. You may have faced a major health battle or you may have lost someone you love seemingly way before their time. Recognizing the shortness of our days can help us redeem them, choosing to spend our time in ways that matter, not just killing time to get to the next cool thing. When we meditate on what God teaches about time, we grow in His wisdom.

Thinking about time doesn't have to be gloomy, even if it is serious. Numbering our days also helps us to notice the goodness of God, His faithfulness, through all our days. Take some time right now, either in the white space on this page or in a journal, to write down three to five ways you've seen God move in your life. This is part of numbering your days.

None of us can control time, but we can grow wise in using time. That may feel like a lesson in study skills, but we mean it in a far more important way. Spending your time wisely and worshiping God go together. Jesus calls you—just like He calls us—to spend the most valuable resource we have on earth to love others, to honor Him, and to get ready for the best time we'll ever spend . . . eternity with Him!

READY TO GO DEEPER? Read James 4:13–15. What do these verses teach you about time? How is God inviting you to respond to the truth you've read today?

Beyond Rule Keeping

Worthy are you, our Lord and God,
to receive glory and honor and power,
for you created all things,
and by your will they existed and were created.

Revelation 4:11

If you've been a Christian for a while, you may have a favorite verse or two. Bethany and I (Kristen) definitely do. The verse I chose for today's devotional is one of my absolute favorites, partly because it's just so powerful and partly because it reminds me what in the world I'm supposed to be doing with my life.

I grew up in an amazing Christian home, at an amazing Christian church, with amazing Christian teaching. And, to be honest, I kinda took that for granted. I also took what I saw as the "rules" of Christianity really seriously. Do this, don't do that, good Christian girls are like this and definitely not like that. Can you relate?

The trouble was, all of this led me to be more of a rule keeper than a Christ worshiper. Don't get me wrong. I loved God back then. But I love Him more every day now that I focus on worshiping Him, not just following a list of dos and don'ts.

I can see why I was drawn, and maybe you've been drawn, to more of a rule-following approach to faith. A lot of us like formulas and boxes we can check off. I read my Bible today. Check. I prayed today. Check. I didn't yell at my parents (even though they were driving me crazy). Check. I'm a good girl, right? Check?

Eventually I had to start asking, *Where is my heart in all this?* I'm doing everything right, but I'm not getting closer to God. *Is it possible to do all the right things and still miss the mark?* I wondered. I figured out that it was, and I didn't want that anymore.

If you want to get beyond living for the rules and checking off the Christian boxes, look with me at Revelation 4:11. This verse tells us that, in heaven, the believers surrounding God's throne cried out,

> Worthy are you, our Lord and God,
>> to receive glory and honor and power,
> for you created all things,
>> and by your will they existed and were created.

Notice that they did *not* say, "O Lord, we did so many good things for you on earth." No way! They were caught up in worship. Worship, not rule keeping, is the secret to living a life of genuine joy in Christ.

We can worship God in many cool ways. We can worship through music—by singing His praise or playing instruments. We can worship through prayer—by spending time thanking God for who He is and what He's done. We can worship through learning—by reading His Word or listening to a good sermon or podcast. We can worship out in nature—by acknowledging

His amazing creativity. Zack and I love visiting national parks, and we've worshiped God at the Grand Canyon (oh my, it was breathtaking) and Zion (gorgeous).

Following a list of rules as your means to godliness won't ultimately lead you to a deeper relationship with Jesus. It may make your life look really good on the outside, but it can also leave your heart empty, judgmental, and rigid. Instead, focus on worshiping God. When you worship, you naturally want to honor God with what you do. Then your choices come from a heart of love. And that's the kind of heart God wants to use to build His kingdom and change the world.

READY TO GO DEEPER? Read Psalm 86:11–12. What does the psalmist pray for here? Spend some time journaling your own prayer about living a life of worship.

DAY 36

Believe It or Not

*Do not be anxious about anything, but in everything
by prayer and supplication with thanksgiving let your
requests be made known to God. And the peace of God,
which surpasses all understanding, will guard your hearts
and your minds in Christ Jesus.*

Philippians 4:6–7

There's nothing quite like reading a great book. We love opening to the first page of a new one or revisiting our old favorites. You may not love reading now (especially if you feel forced to do it for school), but don't give up on it. You have so much to look forward to! Books have changed our lives.

One book that's made a huge impact on both of us is Nancy Leigh DeMoss's *Choosing Gratitude: Your Journey to Joy.* The thirty-day devotional in the back of the book totally helped us too.

Nancy makes this simple but powerful point in her book: "I have learned that in every circumstance that comes my way, I can choose to respond in one of two ways: I can whine or I can worship! And I can't worship without giving thanks. It just isn't possible."[1] We can't choose our circumstances, but we can choose our response. We can whine or worship. We can also worry. Of these three *w*'s, which will make your life better? It's a no-duh question, right? So why do we so often turn to whining or worrying?

Jesus told us, "In the world you will have tribulation. But take heart; I have overcome the world" (John 16:33). The word *tribulation* means trouble or heartache. Life overflows with things that prompt us to worry or whine. Knowing that Jesus overcomes the world enables us to worship instead.

Philippians 4:6–7, today's verses, gives us another amazing reason to worship God. Through the apostle Paul, God tells us not to be anxious about anything, but to focus on prayer and supplication. *Supplication* is a fancy word for humbly making your needs and requests known to your heavenly Father. Jesus also tells us to include gratitude in this. That's the "with thanksgiving" piece.

God doesn't just tell us this because gratitude is a good habit to develop. He actually made our brains to operate best when we give thanks. Here's how it works: Your brain has certain pathways that correspond to particular emotions. Joy goes down one brain pathway, anger down another. God designed our brains so that the pathways for gratitude and worry cannot cross. Your brain cannot be grateful and worried at the same time. What a powerful reason to choose gratitude!

But it gets even better. As we choose gratitude, as we get off the worry or the whining brain highways, we receive God's peace and protection. He literally guards our hearts and minds. And the peace He gives is beyond what we can ask for or imagine. We just *love* that!

Gratitude is like a gate you walk through to get to the other side of tough circumstances, like an arch you walk under to get to the peace and protection of God waiting for you. We highly recommend that you grab a copy of *Choosing Gratitude*, and we pray it will encourage you as much as it did us. And next time you're tempted to worry, write (or voice memo into your phone) five to ten things you're grateful for. Gratitude really does make a world of difference.

READY TO GO DEEPER? Read 1 Thessalonians 5:16–18. What does this passage say about God's will for our lives? How do these verses fit with what you read today?

Shine Bright!

Let your light shine before others, so that they may see your good works and give glory to your Father who is in heaven.

Matthew 5:16

After a basketball practice under the boiling Texas sun, I (Bethany) was relieved when Coach called us to a final huddle. My team formed a tight circle. Since we were prepping for a national competition, I figured Coach would do the talking. Instead, he suggested we take turns sharing words of encouragement with one another.

Cue awkward silence. And more silence. Then crickets-chirping silence.

Let's just say no one was thrilled about this team-building activity.

Totally shocking me, the most unlikely person broke the ice and turned toward me . . .

"I've been watching you. Your Christianity is real to you, and you truly live it out. I want you to know that I'm inspired to do the right thing because of you."

Completely stunned, I said something brilliant like, "Wow, um, thanks."

This person was the last human on the planet I thought would care about how I lived out my faith in Jesus. I never imagined she'd notice me trying to do the right thing. But she *was* watching, and what I did *mattered*.

Someone is always watching. Okay, that came out creepier than I meant it to be. Ha ha. I mean that you and I never know when the world will sit up and take notice. I'm just a regular girl, with normal ups and downs, who loves God. I hadn't been a perfect Christian on the court; I had simply lived out what I believed.

When Jesus urged His disciples, "Let your light shine before others, so that they may see your good works and give glory to your Father who is in heaven," He intended for them—and us—to shine not just in spiritual moments but also in regular activities. Back then, for me that included attending basketball practice, hanging out with my siblings, and doing schoolwork. God called me to let my light shine in everyday life. Today I choose to shine bright whether I'm running errands or directing GirlDefined Ministries, whether I'm drinking coffee with a girlfriend or mentoring someone, whether I'm sweating at the gym or sweating (perhaps less but still sweating) because the Holy Spirit has invited me to give a gospel tract to the barista.

In other words, my entire life is pointed in a particular direction: shining bright for Jesus. Why? Not so others can see I'm a good person, but so they can see God and give Him glory. Wouldn't it be amazing if, when we've all crossed over into eternity, someone told you, "You never knew this, but I watched you and saw your love for Jesus. You're one of the reasons I gave my life to the Lord." Can you imagine?

Sister, let your light shine—and I'm talking shine *bright*—before others. You never know whose life you will change simply because you chose to shine.

READY TO GO DEEPER? Read Matthew 5:43–45. According to this passage, what's one way you can really shine for Jesus? Is this easy or difficult for you? Journal about it, and ask the Holy Spirit for help.

Each of Us Is an Original

*If we live by the Spirit, let us also keep in step with the
Spirit. Let us not become conceited, provoking one another,
envying one another.*

Galatians 5:25–26

We've got five sisters in our family, two sisters-in-law, and our
sweet mama. We don't even have to leave our family to compare
ourselves to other girls! The eight of us may share some traits,
but we're all *so different*. Our body types, our features, the way
our hair grows (or doesn't!), our skin tones. If we let it, comparing ourselves with our own family members could drive us crazy.

And the truth is, we've struggled with the comparison game
way beyond our family circle and certainly beyond how we look.
As a young kid, I (Kristen) remember a neighbor wanting to
compare allowances. I didn't get an allowance, which was a source
of total embarrassment for me! As Bethany and I grew older,
both of us drove old, beat-up cars . . . more embarrassment. The
two of us also compared our basketball skills, who got more attention from guys, who got the opportunity to do this or that.
On and on it went.

It's called the comparison trap for a reason, and we have felt
absolutely trapped by it at some point or another.

We know we're not the only ones. I imagine you've felt tempted to compare yourself to others, online or in real life. The rise of social media means that you can—at any minute—compare yourself to the most talented, beautiful, and popular people, not just around you but from all over the world. It's exhausting!

A fellow blogger, Erin Davis, helped us see that the comparison trap is set by none other than God's enemy:

> He knows that comparing ourselves with others leads to feelings of discouragement, inadequacy, and jealousy. He knows that if he can turn our focus toward those around us, he can easily distract us. . . . Our need to compare wasn't born in the twenty-first century. It isn't simply a result of media that pushes a version of beauty that is impossible to obtain. The enemy has been setting this trap since the beginning. A return back to God's Word shows us that many have been ensnared, often with terrible results.[1]

Thanks to Jesus, we don't have to stay trapped. The lock that keeps us imprisoned to comparison is on *our* side of the door! And we have the key. John 8:32 is clear: "The truth will set you free."

Today's verses help us break the chains of comparison. Take a second and reread Galatians 5:25–26. The apostle Paul uses three powerful words here: *conceited, provoking, envying*. In essence, he's telling us that comparing ourselves with each other, as if one were better and another worse, is the opposite of life in the Spirit. We love how one paraphrase renders Galatians 5:26: "We have far more interesting things to do with our lives. Each of us is an original."[2]

Each of us is an original. Friend, these six words can change your life. Let them! *You are an original*, a masterpiece more precious than the *Mona Lisa* or England's crown jewels.

The truth that we're original masterpieces can set us free and enable us to find far more interesting things to do with our lives than compare ourselves with one another. What are some things you can praise God for instead of staying trapped in comparison? Ask God the Holy Spirit to help you find those things, starting today.

READY TO GO DEEPER? Read Proverbs 14:30. If someone asked you if you wanted perfect health or rotten bones, which would you choose? Seriously! Spend some time talking to God about why so many of us stay trapped in envy and end up feeling rotten. Pray for His help.

DAY 39

The Good Life

Blessed is the man
  who walks not in the counsel of the wicked,
nor stands in the way of sinners,
  nor sits in the seat of scoffers;
but his delight is in the law of the Lord,
  and on his law he meditates day and night.

He is like a tree
  planted by streams of water
that yields its fruit in its season,
  and its leaf does not wither.
In all that he does, he prospers.

Psalm 1:1–3

Do you remember when #Blessed was *everywhere*?

Even people who had no interest in God or the Bible snapped up #Blessed tees, journals, and bedroom decor. Why? Because everyone loves the idea of being blessed. From the beginning of time, people have desired and chased after "the good life."

And that's totally relatable! There's nothing wrong with wanting life to go well. Here's where #Blessed becomes problematic. If we don't know what the good life actually means, we'll never experience God's true blessing. Thankfully, God enables us to understand what it means to be blessed genuinely (not just with a hashtag).

Psalm 1:1–3 gives us a beautiful picture of the good life: a luscious fruitful tree, planted by streams of water and flourishing—not withering—forever. Verse 3 ends with this amazing promise: everything the blessed person does prospers. Wow!

How do we get to this blessed life? Psalm 1:1–3 directs us in this too. To experience God's blessing, we're commanded to reject the counsel of the world, to separate ourselves from those living in sin, to delight in the Word of God, and to think about His truth throughout the day. Let's break each of these down just a bit.

First, we're urged to walk "not in the counsel of the wicked." In other words, don't listen to lies! The world may whisper, "It's not that big of a deal if you cheat on that one exam; you've been good *every other time*." Don't listen! The counsel of the wicked may sound like this: "It doesn't matter how you treat your family; I mean, nobody's *perfect*." Don't listen! The world may promise, "It's okay to sleep with your boyfriend if you really love him." Girl, don't listen! To live a blessed life, we've got to steer clear of the counsel of the wicked. Don't take advice from the world, and don't listen to lies. It's simple, but that doesn't mean it's always easy. We desperately need the Holy Spirit to guide us so that we listen to His truth, not the world's lies.

Psalm 1:1–3 also tells us that, to live the good life, we must not "[stand] in the way of sinners" or "[sit] in the seat of scoffers." What on earth does that mean? It doesn't mean we are to have zero interaction with people who aren't Christians. God calls us to love everyone—Christian or not—and witness to those who don't yet know Jesus. You can't do that while refusing to be with people.

Here's what not standing with sinners or sitting with scoffers *does* mean. It means not spending your time affirming or indulging in sin. A couple examples: Don't hang around while people gossip, even if you're not saying anything. Just walk away. Choose not to spend hours tracking celebrity affairs or horrific crimes. Flip the switch or click away when people scoff at the name of God. Don't just sit there. Again, simple but potentially difficult. But girl, you have the strength of the Spirit and the wisdom to do this.

Finally, Psalm 1:1–3 promises that the blessed life comes for those who delight in God's Word. Consider this: Would your life be more or less blessed if you spent fifteen minutes in God's Word rather than scrolling and tapping? I'm not trying to give you a guilt trip; it's a serious question. If you don't believe your life will be changed by God's Word, of course you won't read it. But if you think there's a chance greater spiritual blessing might come your way, why wouldn't you take it? Try reading a psalm a day, or start with the Gospel accounts of Jesus's life. Tune in tomorrow for more ideas. Sister, what do you have to lose? And what might you have to gain?

READY TO GO DEEPER? Read Job 1:21. Can you be blessed even in losing something you love? Why or why not? Is it possible to bless the Lord, even in loss? Talk to God about it.

DAY 40

Studying Your Bible— and Loving It!

Everyone then who hears these words of mine and does them will be like a wise man who built his house on the rock. And the rain fell, and the floods came, and the winds blew and beat on that house, but it did not fall, because it had been founded on the rock.

Matthew 7:24–25

If you're reading in order, the last devotional you read encouraged you to spend time in God's Word. We gave a couple brief suggestions at the end of that devo, but today I (Kristen) will share with you a simple way to read and interact with God's Word. It's been helpful for me, and I pray it will be for you too.

I originally heard it called the Swedish Method, though it goes by other names online. I honestly haven't been able to figure out whether it came from Sweden or someone named Swedish made it up. Okay, probably not the latter.

Here's what you need: a Bible, a notebook/journal, and something to write with. That's it!

Start with prayer. Maybe you want to thank God for being with you, for saving you and making you part of His family,

His beloved daughter. Then ask the Holy Spirit to speak to you through God's Word.

The next step: read a passage of Scripture (one chapter is ideal) out loud. Yep, out loud. You engage your entire self—brain, body, and spirit—when you read aloud. Now, go back and read the passage again, this time silently and with the express purpose of looking for three things:

1. *Light bulb.* Identify something that stands out—an idea or a statement, anything that jumps off the page. You may find more than one! If you like writing in your Bible, draw a light bulb in the margin. Write down what you notice in your journal.

2. *Question mark.* This is your chance to—you guessed it—write down any questions you have after reading this passage. If you could ask God anything about these verses, what would you ask? Take notes.

3. *Arrow.* Finally, look for ways to apply this passage. What is God inviting you to do in response to this chapter of Scripture? Again, you may find more than one. Write down everything you discover.

Let's try this with the verses from Matthew at the opening of this devotional. If I were practicing the Swedish Method, I might put a light bulb next to "everyone who hears these words of mine and does them will be like a wise man." This is an important idea to me. I might ask the questions, What rain, floods, or wind are beating against my house (my life) right now? How can God's Word help me withstand these? Finally, I might place an arrow next to "it had been founded on the rock," because I want to make sure I'm building on the right foundation.

Typically, I would want to read more than just two verses to understand the context. Also, the richness of God's Word is meant to be savored! I wanted to show you that it's possible to use this method even with small amounts of Scripture. You can carry His light bulb and arrow truths throughout your day, which is another thing God says brings a blessed life. So, get to it, girl!

READY TO GO DEEPER? Read the entire chapter of Matthew 7. Practice the Swedish Method, and talk with God about what you discover.

DAY 41

Better for You

Do not quench the Spirit.

1 Thessalonians 5:19

quench [kwench], verb
1: to put out the light or fire of
2: to bring . . . to an end, typically by satisfying,
cooling, damping or decreasing[1]

If you're on a call and can't hear the person on the other line, what do you do? Yeah, you turn up the volume. However, what do you do if you *don't* want to hear what people are saying on the TV or an online video? In our digital age, you mute them.

We can do a similar thing with God the Holy Spirit's voice in our lives. The apostle Paul describes this as "quenching" the Holy Spirit in 1 Thessalonians 5:19. We can either turn off or turn up the light of God in our hearts. We can decrease the Spirit's fire within us or fan His fire into flames.

So, which are you going to choose? Will you listen to the Spirit or quench His voice?

That may be a question you've never considered before today. That's okay. Today is a great day to decide that you'll attune your mind and heart to the Spirit's voice! To do that, it will help to learn a bit about God the Holy Spirit.

God's Spirit actively moved in the events of history and in people's lives throughout the Old Testament age. Among many other things, He granted gifts to artists and prophets, empowered warriors, and taught people God's ways.

Today, God the Holy Spirit takes an even more personal role in the life of every believer—including you! Ephesians describes this: "In him you also, when you heard the word of truth, the gospel of your salvation, and believed in him, were sealed with the promised Holy Spirit, who is the guarantee of our inheritance until we acquire possession of it, to the praise of his glory" (Eph. 1:13–14). God the Holy Spirit dwells in you as the down payment of God's promise to bring you safely home one day—to live in peace, without pain or heartache, forever for His glory.

The Bible tells us that some of the Spirit's roles in our lives include comforting and helping us, as well as convicting us of sin and guiding us in the way we should go. He strengthens and empowers us, sustains hope in our hearts, enables us to understand God's will for our lives, creates holy character in us, and supernaturally fills us so that we can worship, pray, and use the gifts He's given us to build up others and speak truth into their lives.

See why it might be important that we not quench but rather tune in to the Spirit's voice?

Jesus even told His disciples that it would be *better for them* that He leave and the Spirit come. Just before His death, Jesus said, "It is to your advantage that I go away, for if I do not go away, the Helper [the Spirit] will not come to you. But if I go, I will send him to you" (John 16:7). That's astonishing! Jesus laid down His life so that we could be sealed, protected, guided, helped, comforted, convicted, and empowered by God's Spirit.

That. Is. Amazing.

The world is systematically trying to quench the Spirit of God's voice. People put God on mute because they want to do "what [is] right in their own eyes" (Judg. 17:6). Don't join them! Pray today—and every day—that you will hear the Spirit's voice and obey what He says. We're praying and striving to do the same.

READY TO GO DEEPER? Read Romans 8. Try the Swedish Method again! Look for specific ways God the Holy Spirit's work is described. Journal a prayer to hear God's voice better each day.

DAY 42

Worth the Wait

Therefore the LORD waits to be gracious to you,
and therefore he exalts himself to show mercy
to you.
For the LORD is a God of justice;
blessed are all those who wait for him.

Isaiah 30:18

If you know anything about my (Bethany's) story, you know that I'm acquainted with waiting. Even though I desired to get married for as long as I can remember, God asked me to wait until I was thirty years old to marry Dāv. Since I waited until marriage for my first-ever kiss, I waited thirty years for that too. Sister, I know how hard waiting can be.

You may be waiting for high school or college to be over so that you can get on with *real* life. You may be waiting for that amazing guy to come into your life or for that perfect job opportunity. The reality is, we do a lot of waiting in life—not just for big things but for a zillion mundane things too. How many hours, on average, do you think people spend waiting in lines at medical offices and government agencies (hmm . . . ever been to the DMV)? There's a reason the English language includes the term *waiting room*! We wait—a lot.

And we don't have super positive associations with waiting, do we? How many people *love* waiting rooms? Yep. Zero. It's kinda crazy, then, that our verse for today tells us "blessed are all those who wait." Come again?

Isaiah 30:18 encourages us to wait, but to wait with purpose—to wait *for* God. And this verse includes something even more surprising. Did you catch in the first part of this verse that "the Lord *waits* to be gracious to you" (emphasis added)? What on earth does that mean? Is God holding back until we figure out how to wait well? By no means!

Let's look at the definitions of *wait* and see what we find. Yes, waiting can include remaining "inactive . . . until something expected happens," but that's just one definition. *Waiting* also means "to be available or in readiness, to continue as one is in expectation of."[1]

God isn't hanging out, inactively waiting. Instead, He's available, ready to be gracious to you, eager to show you mercy, poised to bring justice. We're blessed when we learn to wait in the same way, to anticipate God's movement in our lives, to eagerly look out for His mercy, to be available for His purposes and plans. This is the kind of waiting God models for us and invites us to learn.

Sometimes we may be called to wait "inactively," but I'd venture to say those occasions are relatively few. Even when I've been waiting for a migraine to pass, curled up in bed, I can wait in anticipation and in prayer. When I'm stuck in line, I can wait while tapping my foot in frustration, or I can wait—like Isaiah 30:18 instructs—on the Lord, using my time to send an encouraging text to someone or revisit a verse I read in my morning quiet time.

Proverbs 3:5–6 highlights one of the most amazing lessons I've learned as a result of waiting—trust. Without the many years of waiting I've done, I never would have grown to love and treasure this passage as much as I do; subscribers to our blog over at GirlDefined.com know these are some of my ultimate favorite verses!

> Trust in the LORD with all your heart,
>> and do not lean on your own understanding.
> In all your ways acknowledge him,
>> and he will make straight your paths.

As I've learned to wait better, to be anticipating and eager and *with God* in my waiting, He's enabled me to trust Him so much more. He's made the way before me clearer. If you want to trust God, don't fight the waiting. Instead, learn—like I'm still learning—to wait well. As we wait for Him, our loving God will bless us with grace, mercy, and justice.

READY TO GO DEEPER? Read Proverbs 3:5–6 again. Rewrite these verses in your own words. Ask God to help you understand how waiting and trusting fit together.

Can You Read?

Great peace have those who love your law;
nothing can make them stumble.
I hope for your salvation, O LORD,
and I do your commandments.
My soul keeps your testimonies;
I love them exceedingly.

Psalm 119:165–67

I (Kristen) don't enjoy doing dishes. They're *never-ending*. I just clear the sink, and then someone puts a dirty glass on the counter. Argh!

Anyways . . . One day I was standing at my kitchen sink, listening to a podcast with Jen Wilkin to make my chores more interesting (great method, BTW—I highly recommend it), when something she said struck me. Since I didn't write it down verbatim, here's a paraphrase: We're in big trouble. We may not be illiterate in the normal sense, but Bible illiteracy is rampant.[1]

Bible illiteracy . . . what? I had never even heard of that!

Here's what it means. Tons of us spend our lives in church but never learn how to read the Bible for ourselves. We don't have a foundational knowledge of God's Word, the kind of understanding that allows us to know what we believe and why we believe it. We identify a person who cannot read words as illiterate. We are *biblically illiterate* when we can't read our Bibles, let's say, outside of a social media or verse-of-the-day format.

Don't get me wrong! I love getting verse-of-the-day updates or seeing uplifting posts that refocus my mind on Jesus. But you and I are biblically illiterate if this, and maybe a message at church on Sunday, is all we take in from week to week.

Here's the thing, girl. We've got to get back to the truth that we read the Bible to discover who God is. The Bible isn't about us! It's about God. Then come the truths of how God relates to us (with everlasting love) and how we relate to God (with worship). When we grow in biblical literacy—when we understand what God's Word says about Him and how we are to respond—we're transformed into who God created us to be.

Today I'd like to challenge you to start developing biblical literacy. One of the ways you can do this is by sticking with one book of the Bible. Instead of jumping around from verse to verse, start at the beginning of one book of the Bible and keep reading it until you finish. Don't think about how long it will take or has taken you to get through a biblical book. Treat it like . . . a book. It would be crazy to read a sentence on every other page of a novel and think you'll understand the story, yet that's kinda what some of us do with our Bibles.

God has written a beautiful love story about who He is and His redemptive plan for humanity. It's contained in the pages of your Bible, from Genesis through Revelation. The story includes passion and intrigue, war and worship. It's the story of God's rescue mission, His redemptive love. If you've never read the full story, how can you understand it?

It may be difficult for you to understand some things you read. Relatable! I've totally been there myself, and that's why I'm so grateful for solid commentaries, Bible dictionaries, and other tools. When I'm reading a book like Numbers or Ezekiel, you can bet I'm turning to some study tools for help.

Now, back to my challenge for today. Will you start your journey of Bible literacy by "staying put" with a book of the Bible? If you want to challenge yourself even further, maybe start with Matthew and make it your goal to read the entire New Testament, start to finish. Sure, it might take you a long time. But what better way to spend your time than getting to know the God who saved you!

Let's not be counted among the women who don't know what we believe or why we believe it. Instead, let's be women who build on a solid foundation, so that when the winds and storms of life come (and they will!), we won't be shaken.

READY TO GO DEEPER? Start reading a book of the Bible today! And if you want to learn more, check out Jen Wilkin's book *Women of the Word: How to Study the Bible with Both Our Hearts and Our Minds.*[2]

A Different Kind of Party Girl

Contribute to the needs of the saints and seek to show hospitality.

Romans 12:13

Some people think I (Bethany) am a little too zealous when it comes to hosting social gatherings. They can't imagine why I'm usually one of the first people to volunteer my apartment to host our friends' game night, our church's life group meetings, or a themed party, shower, or hangout. "Don't you hate getting the house ready?" they ask. "Isn't it kinda hard when you don't have that much space?"

Okay, so maybe I don't love cleaning, but I do love hostessing. I'm totally into planning a theme and finding cute decor to match. Putting together a plan for the night's activities excites me, and I love welcoming people to our apartment—even if it is on the small side—and making them feel at home. It's important to me to practice this kind of hospitality.

Some people have a special gift for making others feel welcomed and loved in their homes. You probably know the kind of people I'm talking about. You feel warm, cozy, and at ease when you're in their house, even when nothing special is going on. I want to be one of those people! I want others to love coming to my place because they can be themselves there, and they know they're safe and accepted. That's one major reason I *practice* hospitality. It's something I want to get better and better at, so I practice.

But there's another—even more significant—reason I choose to be hospitable. The Bible commands it! Our verse for today teaches that we honor God by contributing to the needs of the saints and showing hospitality (Rom. 12:13).

Let's put those two things together by considering a couple questions. How many people do you think need a place to be real, to feel safe, and to be loved? How many people would be blessed to come into a home where they are fully welcomed and accepted? How many people do you imagine have never experienced this? Maybe you've never felt this way in any home, even your own. If that's your story, I am so sorry; my heart hurts with you. No matter what you've experienced so far, you can be part of turning the tide in your life and in the lives of others.

And you don't have to wait until you have your own place to practice hospitality. If you have a friend over, seek to show hospitality, just like our verse for today urges. You can make people feel loved and at home in your space through simple things like serving them food and drinks, making sure the bathroom is clean in case someone needs to use it, asking if there's anything your guest needs, listening to them . . . basically thinking of their needs above your own. You can also practice hospitality by celebrating other people. Be the one to throw a surprise party or initiate your friends getting together, and make it fabulous when you do.

While you're practicing this, keep in mind God's Word through Peter: "Show hospitality to one another without grumbling" (1 Pet. 4:9). You may not be thrilled to clean the bathroom, but can you do it without complaining to honor God and show love to others? If I can, I know you can too!

READY TO GO DEEPER? Read 3 John 1:8. According to this verse, what is another major reason we are called to show hospitality? In today's culture, what would working together for truth look like?

DAY 45

Good at What He Does

He who is the blessed and only Sovereign, the King of kings and Lord of lords, who alone has immortality, who dwells in unapproachable light, whom no one has ever seen or can see. To him be honor and eternal dominion.

1 Timothy 6:15–16

Over the last couple years, the two of us have recorded some videos answering assumptions people make about us. We invited people to send us direct messages with their assumptions on social media and . . . *wow!* The digital world has developed some strong opinions about us, ranging from the super serious—we only hang out with people who have the exact same Christian views as we do (absolutely *not* true)—to the silly yet fun—we swap clothes with all five of our sisters (yep, that one's truer than true). Some people assumed we always get along or we're always cheerful and never frustrated with each other. Um . . .

Girl, we're real people! We definitely struggle with kindness toward each other sometimes. Usually it's the most difficult when one—or both—of us falls into the control trap. We're both strong-willed girls who like things done a certain way. When either of us gets too focused on controlling how something should go, things go south pretty quickly.

The problems with trying to control your life and the lives of others stack up quickly. Controlling people are difficult to be around, aren't they? When one of us is in control-girl mode, we're more anxious, less understanding, and basically a pill to work with. Who wants that? And yet we find ourselves trying to control things all too often.

It's understandable why so many girls want to control things; being out of control can feel super scary. But how well do any of us control things? Not so well, my friend.

The Bible tells us that only God has the "power that enables him to bring everything under his control" (Phil. 3:21).[1] The name *Sovereign Lord*, used over three hundred times in Scripture, identifies God as the source of all authority. *Nothing* is outside of His control. One of our favorite sources for Bible help, Desiring God.org, helps us understand this: "There are no limits to God's rule. This is part of what it means to be God. He is sovereign over the whole world, and everything that happens in it. He is never helpless, never frustrated, never at a loss."[2] Wow! Isn't it amazing and comforting to know that God is in control . . . always?

The verses we chose for today's devotional make another important point. Not only is God in control, but He's also very good at what He does. Look back at 1 Timothy 6:15. Our God is the "blessed and only Sovereign." When either of us is trying to clamp down and take control of a situation, we are far from being a blessing to others. What about you? Are you able to love others selflessly when you're in control-girl mode?

We know it can be tough to trust. Sometimes everything seems out of control, and you may wonder if God really is the blessed and only Sovereign. Your parents' divorce, friends betraying you, your boyfriend walking out, school shootings . . . is God in control of all this? Yes, sister, He is still sovereign when everything hurts. Just think about what He did on the cross: He took something completely horrific, something that looked like the very end of hope itself, and turned it for good. The enemy intends sickness, pain, and sin to work for his evil purposes. But God sovereignly turns even these tragic things to work together for the good of those who love Him, just like Romans 8:28 promises.

You can trust your blessed Sovereign Lord with your past, your present, and your future. You can let go of the need to control. We're working on this, too, surrendering control to the only One who can control well and control perfectly. We pray you'll join us in this!

READY TO GO DEEPER? Read Daniel 2:20–21. According to these verses, what does God sovereignly direct? Is it easy or difficult for you to surrender control? Journal your prayer about it.

DAY 46

You're My Only Hope

For God alone, O my soul, wait in silence,
for my hope is from him.
He only is my rock and my salvation,
my fortress; I shall not be shaken.
On God rests my salvation and my glory;
my mighty rock, my refuge is God.

Trust in him at all times, O people;
pour out your heart before him;
God is a refuge for us.

Psalm 62:5–8

Silence doesn't come easy for me (Kristen). Writing, speaking, recording videos, answering GirlDefined emails . . . communication is my job! Apart from my work, I also love talking to family and friends, listening to music and podcasts, basically doing non-silent things.

And yet . . .

God tells me that certain things can't be enjoyed or experienced except through silence. That's a challenge for me, especially in today's super-loud world. I don't know about you, but to find true silence, I have to deliberately plan. Even then, it seems like someone always starts doing übernoisy yard work right when I'm trying to quiet my mind.

Psalm 62 paints a beautiful picture of a heart at rest in God. The psalmist waits in silence for God, his only hope. King David wrote Psalm 62, using words like *fortress* and *refuge* to describe the Lord. David started his journey as a warrior, not a palace-raised prince; these weren't just words to him. For people who have been in battle, fortresses and refuges really matter. Both are safe places, places of protection and relief from the fury of combat.

I imagine that you've felt beat up by life once or twice. You've probably faced days that felt more like war than anything else, more like battle with family and friends than happily ever after. And the reality is, war *is* going on all around us in the heavenly realms. God's Word tell us, "Your adversary the devil prowls around like a roaring lion, seeking someone to devour" (1 Pet. 5:8). That's why we need to find our refuge and safety in God alone. Look back at Psalm 62 and notice its reminder: He only is our Mighty Rock. In Him, I will not be shaken—and neither will you. To experience this, though, we've got to get away from the noise of the world now and then. Are you picking up what I'm putting down, sister?

To learn silence and stillness, start with small amounts of time. You might consider setting a timer for one minute. For those of us who haven't been accustomed to being quiet and still, this might feel pretty long! You're not simply being silent for the sake of silence, though. It's important—and helpful—to remember that your silence is meant to give you a chance to focus on God alone. Use the silence to think about Him!

Maybe try your minute of silence after you've read some Scripture for the day. Let the words you read about God flow back over you. This not only honors God but also cements His truth in your mind and heart. So many times I've breezed through the day and completely forgotten anything I might have read in my Bible. I don't want that! Taking time to be still helps me fix my eyes on Jesus more throughout the whole day.

Psalm 62 also offers us an amazing invitation during our stillness. "Pour out your heart" to God, my friend, "casting all your anxieties on him, because he cares for you" (1 Pet. 5:7). He cares for you. He cares about you. He cares about all the zillions of things warring around you. Pour out your heart to Him and "trust in him at all times," just as Psalm 62:8 encourages.

READY TO GO DEEPER? Set a timer for one minute and practice being still and silent with God. Remember, He is a safe place (refuge). You can pour out your heart to Him! After the timer rings, journal about this experience.

On Purpose

For we are his workmanship, created in Christ Jesus for
good works, which God prepared beforehand, that we
should walk in them.

Ephesians 2:10

Typing "What is the purpose of my life" into a computer's search bar yields over 2,280,000,000 results in 0.58 seconds. When we did this, the top hit came from the University of Minnesota's "Taking Charge of Your Health and Wellbeing" web page. Not sure why that struck us as so surprising; maybe we didn't imagine Minnesota had greater insight into the secrets to life than any other state.

Props to the Minnesotans, though. The website included some helpful and straightforward definitions: "Your life purpose consists of the central motivating aims of your life—the reasons you get up in the morning. Purpose can guide life decisions, influence behavior, shape goals, offer a sense of direction, and create meaning. For some people, purpose is connected to vocation—meaningful, satisfying work."[1]

We can understand why this website, as well as over 2,280,000,000 others, included this discussion of life purpose, meaning, and direction. People under twenty-five, part of Generation Z, have been simultaneously described as "identity nomads," "True Gen," and the most anxious and insecure generation yet.[2] If your head is spinning trying to reconcile all of that, you're not alone! It can be confusing to be a girl in today's day and age. Few things seem solid anymore; fluidity and change are praised, even when they seem to create more problems than they solve.

Girl, you can take this to the bank: you have a reason to get up every morning. You have a purpose that can guide your decisions and shape your goals. You have meaningful and satisfying work ahead of you. Jesus promises this! Look back at today's verse. Good works have been prepared for you.

When you think of good works, don't think simply good versus bad things. Yes, that's an important part of it. But good works mean even more than that. They mean the works only you can do—remember, these were prepared for *you*. Your God-given work benefits not just you but also the whole world. Theologian Frederick Buechner puts it this way: "The place God calls you to is the place where your deep gladness and the world's deep hunger meet."[3] Your purpose isn't some dreary thing waiting out there for you. God has plans for you that are good—plans for your purpose and a wonderful future.

And even though many people your age feel anxious about what they're supposed to do, and when, and how, you don't have to. Even if deciding on a college, career, or relationship weighs heavily on you (and believe us, we've been there), you aren't required to carry that weight. You can decide to trust God; He *will* reveal the good works He's planned for you in Jesus.

For you to trust God with your purpose, it's important to know that you were created not just for a purpose, but also *on purpose.* God made you for a reason! You are His workmanship. The original Greek word for *workmanship* means "masterpiece." You are an original masterpiece, made on purpose for the purpose of fulfilling, kingdom-building work that only you can do. If that isn't something amazing to get up for in the morning, we don't know what is. You don't have to wait until you graduate—or for anything else—to start doing the good works He's planned for you. If you ask, God will guide you to something, even today, that you can do to bring the good news of the gospel into the world. Go after it, girl!

READY TO GO DEEPER? Read Isaiah 43. Try the Swedish Method again. Now look at verse 7. Why did God make and form you? Talk to God about what good works He has planned for you.

DAY 48
No Other Gods

These men have taken their idols into their hearts, and set the stumbling block of their iniquity before their faces.

Ezekiel 14:3

I (Bethany) have recommended certain books over and over again; they're just *that* good. Elyse Fitzpatrick's *Idols of the Heart: Learning to Long for God Alone* definitely falls into that category. I first read it years ago, and I'm not exaggerating to say it changed my life. Elyse writes about how easily defeat and discouragement can creep into our lives because we, like the people Ezekiel 14:3 identifies, "have taken [our] idols into [our] hearts." It's crummy to acknowledge, but because *I* have taken idols into my own heart, I've battled habitual sins that have caused unnecessary pain for myself and for others.

Every single one of us was created to worship. Even people who don't choose to follow God make this clear. They're sports fanatics or fashion devotees, they work eighty-hour weeks or hook up with lots of people. In other words, they worship pleasure or success or self. All of us worship; if it's not God Almighty, it will be someone or something else.

I go to church regularly and read my Bible. It would be easy for me to assume I don't have idols in my heart. You may feel that way too. Below are some simple questions that can help us evaluate whether we've taken idols into our hearts.

- What do you daydream about; where do your thoughts naturally go when you're alone?
- What do you complain about most?
- What worries you?
- What disappoints you most?
- Where does your spending money go?
- What pops up on your social media feed?
- Where do you turn when you're hurting? Do you head for the fridge? Call a friend? Flip on the TV or computer?[1]

Answering these questions honestly can help us see where we may be tempted to worship. At different points in my life, I have taken relationships with guys, how I look (or frustration over how I don't look), and even my own rules-driven Christianity as idols of my heart. Even good things like running a ministry or being a there-for-everyone friend can become idols if I start focusing my life more on them than on cultivating my relationship with Jesus.

Surrendering our idols to God so He can remove them can feel painful, like weeds being ripped out from the garden of my heart. But I don't want weeds there. I want to "keep [my] heart with all vigilance, for from it flow the springs of life" (Prov. 4:23). Our lives are changed by what we worship.

Take some time today to journal your responses to the questions in this devotional. Don't miss this chance; let God transform your heart by removing the idols that have taken root. Pray with me: "Create in me a clean heart, O God, and renew a right spirit within me; I will worship you alone."[2]

READY TO GO DEEPER? Read Isaiah 45:20. According to this passage, not only is worshiping idols sin, it's also pointless. Talk to God about one idol you may have in your heart. Why is it pointless to hold on to that idol? Ask God for His help in letting go.

Something Lost, Something Better Found

And you shall remember the whole way that the LORD your God has led you these forty years in the wilderness, that he might humble you, testing you to know what was in your heart, whether you would keep his commandments or not.

Deuteronomy 8:2

I (Kristen) had waited until the last minute again. I needed a birthday gift for my sweet little sis, and I needed it ASAP. I hit up a nearby clothing store and found a couple adorable tops for her. Perfect. Breathing a sigh of relief, I rushed home to get ready for our family party.

After setting down my bags, I reached into my purse to grab my phone.

No phone.

I must have left it in the car. I went outside to check.

No phone.

That sinking feeling hit me. I must have left it at the store.

Logging on to the program linking my laptop and my phone, I zeroed in on my phone's location. Whoa, this might work out. The phone was still there!

Of course, I immediately called the store using Zack's phone. After six looonnnggg minutes of being on hold, a customer service rep told me no one had turned in a cell phone. Even though I went back to the store to look myself, I just sensed it was gone for good.

And it was.

Up until this point, I wouldn't have said I was attached to my electronics. If stuff got broken or lost, I wasn't super bummed. This time, though, it felt like part of me was gone. Not having instant access to my stuff—texts, apps, photos, music—hit me . . . hard. For the first time, I realized how incredibly dependent I had become on my phone.[1]

Because I couldn't get a new phone for a couple days, I had to do without one. To be honest, those felt like some of the longest days of my life! Instead of turning to my phone to shoot a quick text, I had to communicate a different way. Instead of scrolling on my apps when I had a spare minute, I had to sit there quietly. I was shocked by how still and silent things were without my phone.

If you had lost your phone that day, not me, you may have experienced something totally different. I imagine a lot of girls would have faced what I did, though: a realization that my phone usage said a lot about the state of my heart.

Deuteronomy 8:2, the verse I chose for today's devotional, talks about how God revealed what was in His people's hearts. Now, I'm not saying God "made" me lose my cell phone. I'm only saying He used that test (think *trial* here more than exam) to show me how much I treasured my phone and where that had taken me.

Instead of engaging in meaningful conversations with people, I would often turn to my phone. Instead of using my time wisely, I ended up doing something totally pointless on an app. Instead of having a focused Bible and prayer time, I got distracted by the buzz of my phone.

If you lost your phone today, what do you think you might learn about your own heart? I'm not setting a trap for you with that question; I'm genuinely trying to help you sort this out *before* you face a trial that forces you to see what's in your heart.

Even though I lost my phone, I found something far better during that experience. I found that a big part of my heart could be turned back to God. The part I had given to my phone I could refocus on Him. It wasn't an easy lesson, but I'm so grateful I found something of eternal value in losing my phone. Sister, you can find the same, without losing something. I pray that you do!

READY TO GO DEEPER? Read Matthew 6:21. What does this verse say about your heart and what you treasure? How does this relate to what you read today? Pray about it.

Teach Us To . . .

> *Our Father in heaven,*
> *hallowed be your name.*
> *Your kingdom come,*
> *your will be done,*
>   *on earth as it is in heaven.*
> *Give us this day our daily bread,*
> *and forgive us our debts,*
>   *as we also have forgiven our debtors.*
> *And lead us not into temptation,*
>   *but deliver us from evil.*
>
>   *Matthew 6:9–13*

Picture this: you can time travel and spend one hour with Jesus (okay, so this is slightly corny, but just go with us). There's only one rule about your time. To get this chance, you have to ask Jesus, at some point, to teach you something. What would you ask Him?

Jesus's disciples actually found themselves in a situation like this, minus the time travel. Yeah, we kinda set you up, but we're pretty sure you figured that out! Okay, back to the important stuff . . . we find the disciples' story recorded in Luke 11. "Now Jesus was praying in a certain place, and when he finished, one of his disciples said to him, 'Lord, teach us to pray ...'" (Luke 11:1).

We're not sure what you would ask Jesus to teach you, but healing the sick and walking on water seem, well, a little more significant than learning how to pray. Isn't prayer just talking to God? That's certainly an important part of it! But have you ever stopped to consider what to say when you talk to God?

The disciples obviously thought they could learn something about prayer from Jesus. They had been with Him for about three years at this point; if they could have simply "picked up" how to pray by watching, we're pretty sure they would've done it. Also, we think it's awesome that Jesus didn't turn to the disciples and say, "Seriously? You don't know this by now?" Instead, Luke 11:2 tells us Jesus replied,

> When you pray, say:
>> Father, hallowed be your name.
>> Your kingdom come ...

He then gave them what we call the Lord's Prayer as an outline for how to pray.

If you've never been taught how to pray—and the reality is, a ton of people in the Church have never been taught—Jesus gives us the perfect lesson, broken down into bite-sized chunks. Start with praising God for who He is—your heavenly Father, holy and set apart (this is what *hallowed* means). Next, acknowledge that His ways are best, that His will is what you want:

>> Your kingdom come,
>> your will be done,
>>> on earth as it is in heaven. (Matt. 6:10)

157

In heaven, God's will is done instantly. The angels don't discuss whether to follow God; they obey! Jesus teaches us to do this too.

We learn to ask for our needs next, what Jesus's prayer describes as our "daily bread." It's essential to note that Jesus doesn't encourage us to ask for a year's worth of bread. The future isn't in our hands; when we humbly focus on today and live in the present, we can trust and serve God more completely.

Jesus taught His disciples to ask for forgiveness and to forgive others when they pray too:

> and forgive us our debts,
>   as we also have forgiven our debtors. (v. 12)

It's astonishing that God tells us to pray as if we've *already* forgiven the people who have hurt us. This is super convicting! It's easy to hold grudges and stay bitter. But we've been forgiven of so, so much, and Jesus enables us to forgive those who have sinned against us.

The disciples' lesson on prayer—and ours—finishes with these final words:

> And lead us not into temptation,
>   but deliver us from evil. (v. 13)

Friend, we need this every day! The world overflows with temptations and evils. Only God can deliver us from them all.

Maybe you've heard the Lord's Prayer before today but never really thought about what it means or how it might lead you to pray. We invite you to take some time today and follow Jesus's pattern of prayer: start with praising God for who He is, recognize His lordship in your life, pray about your daily needs, ask for forgiveness for what you've done today that's gone against God's will, forgive others, and pray for His help to face temptation.

You've learned well today; we're proud of you!

READY TO GO DEEPER? Read Luke 11:1–13. What else does Jesus say about prayer in this passage? Journal about how you can start implementing those things into your prayer life.

The Kind of Fear That Leads to Life

*The law of your mouth is better to me
than thousands of gold and silver pieces.*

Psalm 119:72

Unbearably hot. That's the reality of a Texas summer. Those are the days I (Bethany) am so glad God gave us water, not just to drink but to swim in too. Growing up, one of my family's favorite summertime activities was piling as many siblings and friends as possible into our van, throwing tubes and toys and towels into the back, and heading to the river. Sweet memories, my friend!

One such day ended rather differently than most. I had totally enjoyed working on my tan as I lounged on the rocky riverbank, relaxing on the water in a floatie, and having sister chats with my sibs. That part = fabulous. And then I remembered I had forgotten to take my favorite silver necklace off before leaving the house. No!

Though I tore apart my beach bag and scoured the riverbank (and I'm talking searched for several hours), I never recovered the necklace. It was gone for good.

As we drove home, disappointment hung over me like a gray storm cloud. I was seriously bummed! Then a verse I had memorized that very month popped into my head. It's the verse I chose for today's devotional:

> The law of your mouth is better to me
> than thousands of gold and silver pieces. (Ps. 119:72)

Meditating on this verse didn't make me feel guilty about missing my necklace or wishing I hadn't lost it. Instead, it caused me to think about how much I really believed the Word of God I had memorized. And not just believed in my mind, but believed to the point that I lived out His truth. You know what I mean? I can say I believe a lot of things, but if my life doesn't line up with what I claim, how much do I actually believe them?

Was God's law really better to me than riches? Do I search for the truth as intently as I searched for my necklace at the river? Proverbs 2:1–5 talks about this very thing.

> If you receive my words,
>   and treasure up my commandments with you,
> making your ear attentive to wisdom
>   and inclining your heart to understanding;
> yes, if you call out for insight
>   and raise your voice for understanding,
> if you seek it like silver
>   and search for it as for hidden treasures,
> then you will understand the fear of the LORD
>   and find the knowledge of God.

When we seek God's truth, when we listen closely and treasure His truth in our hearts, we not only know God more, but we also fear Him more too. This may confuse some people; I definitely needed help understanding the fear of the Lord. To fear the Lord isn't to be scared of Him like I might be scared of swimming with sharks. The Bible tells us clearly:

> The fear of the LORD leads to life,
>   and whoever has it rests satisfied. (Prov. 19:23)

The fear of the Lord must be a *way* different kind of fear than we normally experience!

The fear of the Lord includes taking God more seriously than anything else; it means respecting Him and longing for Him above all. I appreciate how Erik Thoennes explains it on *The Gospel Coalition Podcast*: "A true fear of the Lord realizes you can't run from God, and the only option is to run to him. When you do, you find the embracing arms of a loving Father."[1]

Sister, there are lots of things we can treasure, a million things we can search for (hello, Internet), but we have only one loving Father. Wisdom and the fear of the Lord keep us running to God, not away from Him and to other things. Please take a moment right now and journal about this. Ask yourself, How much do I really value God's truth? Do I genuinely seek it? Talk to Jesus about what it means to fear the Lord, and ask God the Holy Spirit for help respecting Him above everything else. Let's commit today to living out what we say we believe. You in?

READY TO GO DEEPER? The fear of the Lord is a big topic. Choose a podcast or blog from www.thegospelcoalition.org to help you understand it more. I'm learning too!

The Right Kind of Influencer

Let no one despise you for your youth, but set the believers an example in speech, in conduct, in love, in faith, in purity.

1 Timothy 4:12

Girls in today's day and age want influence more than ever. Influencer has become not only a desirable job for young adults but also a source of intense stress and envy. Someone who has more influence must have a better life, right?

We're not convinced. For influence and the good life to go hand in hand, we have to be headed in the right direction. Will having thousands of followers influenced by our wardrobe, makeup tips, or product contracts bring us more peace and joy? Will more likes and comments actually bring us true satisfaction?

The truth is, regardless of your friendship circle or social media following, we're *all* influencers. Think about it. Being an influencer simply means you're influencing someone else. We all do this on a daily basis, whether or not we realize it. So, what if you decided to be an influencer for things that will last, things that actually help you and others enjoy the life you crave? What if you were a girl who sets trends that stretch into eternity?

The Bible tells us there are ways to influence others that don't fade with a fashion season or stage of life. Scripture also says that young women can do this in powerful ways. While some older people look down on high school students or young adults— *What do they know? They're only kids*—that's *not* how Jesus sees you. God used the apostle Paul to write the words in 1 Timothy 4:12, "Let no one despise you for your youth." Just because you're younger doesn't mean you can't have *massive* influence.

How do you do it? Our verse for today paves the way: "Set the believers an example in speech, in conduct, in love, in faith, in purity." In other words, be a trendsetter by your example in five specific areas: how you speak, what you do, how you love, what you believe, and how you honor God by pursuing purity.

If you want real, lasting influence, let Jesus transform the way you talk. Listen to the Holy Spirit and act in obedience to His Word. Don't simply go with the flow. Instead, *decide* that your life will flow in God's direction. Choose to influence people with your love more than your clothes or the products you could get paid to represent. Set a faith trend by actually living out what you believe—not just saying you're a Christian but genuinely living like Jesus and obeying His Word. Great influence comes with great holiness, so let God purify your heart, mind, and choices.

You don't have to wait until you're older or have a blue checkmark on your social media profile to be an influencer. You don't have to get paid to set trends. You can start today by setting an example with your speech, conduct, love, faith, and purity.

One final thought: to do this, you actually have to want it. If you want influence in the world more than in eternity, you'll keep chasing affirmation . . . forever. Decide today what you will do. "If serving the LORD seems undesirable to you, then choose for yourselves this day whom you will serve.... But as for me and my household, we will serve the LORD" (Josh. 24:15).[1] What about you?

READY TO GO DEEPER? Read 1 Corinthians 11:1. What does Paul tell the church at Corinth to do? Could you tell someone to follow you as you follow Christ? What kind of example are you setting right now?

What's on Your Mind?

For where your treasure is, there your heart will be also.

Matthew 6:21

Both of us spent a lot of time thinking about guys in our teens and early twenties. We talked about crushes with friends. We daydreamed about guys we liked. We imagined romantic encounters. I (Kristen) even had a spot in my closet designated to practice kissing. True story!

As people, we don't just spend time on things; we spend thoughts on them too. Have you ever considered that? Most of us don't spend a whole lot of energy pondering what we think about, but the Bible encourages us to do that very thing. What we think about tells us a whole lot about who we really are.

Jesus spoke our verse for today as part of the Sermon on the Mount. Basically, thousands of people followed Jesus onto a hillside, where he taught them about real-life issues ranging from prayer and fasting to adultery and judging others. Jesus also addressed the topic of the heart.

In the Bible, when you see the phrase "the heart," think beyond the organ in your body that pumps blood. The Bible defines the heart as the source of the "springs of life" (Prov. 4:23) that includes not only the emotions but also the mind and the will (your decision-making and intention-keeping faculties). Matthew 6:21 says, "For where your treasure is, there your heart will be also."

You and I think about what we treasure most. That's why I spent so much time thinking about guys when I was younger. I treasured them. Some of my thoughts were of the totally normal, growing-up-and-being-romantically-interested-in-boys kind. But some of my thoughts went down a darker path of sexual fantasy. Both Bethany and I have written about struggling with sexual temptation in our book *Sex, Purity, and the Longings of a Girl's Heart* and on our blog. If this is something you've faced, we highly recommend you grab a copy of the book or search the archives on our blog at www.GirlDefined.com/archives.

Maybe you haven't dealt with that particular temptation in your thought life. Maybe you treasure sports, fitness, or being super strong, so your thoughts drift toward comparing yourself to other athletes or to girls who are skinnier or stronger than you. Your thoughts might be consumed with the cute clothes other people can afford to buy, the mansion-like houses they live in, or the cool opportunities they get and you don't (vacations, college, marriage).

Our thoughts can go in so many different directions, and a lot of those directions aren't so pretty. Am I right? That's why it's so essential that, as Christian girls, we not only consider what we're thinking about but also let God transform our thought lives. Romans 12:2 addresses this clearly: "Do not be conformed to this world, but be transformed by the renewal of your mind, that by testing you may discern what is the will of God, what is good and acceptable and perfect." In other words, let God transform you by changing the way you think.

The promises attached to this verse are powerful. We'll be able to discern between what's good and bad, what's acceptable and harmful, what's perfect and flawed. Romans 12:2 also gives us clear direction in how to avoid the harmful stuff: don't be conformed to this world.

The world will fill our minds if we let it. We can go an entire day—maybe even whole weeks—without choosing what to think about. Our feeds or our classwork, streaming movies or music will gladly fill our minds to overflowing. We can deliberately choose differently, though. We can turn our thoughts to God! When we treasure God, our hearts and minds naturally follow. Let's not just default to thinking about "whatever." Instead, let's be intentional with what's on our minds.

READY TO GO DEEPER? Read 2 Corinthians 10:5. What does it mean to "take every thought captive"? How might this fit with not being conformed to the world and treasuring God in your mind and heart?

I Can't Wait

As the deer pants for streams of water,
so my soul pants for you, my God.
My soul thirsts for God, for the living God.
When can I go and meet with God?

Psalm 42:1–2[1]

I (Bethany) move through life at a very particular speed, and that speed is *fast*. I walk fast, think fast, talk fast, eat fast. I even grew fast. I'm a mover and a shaker, girl! But there's one time of the day I really wish I didn't move so fast: when I sit down to spend time with God.

There have been way too many days when I've zoomed through my quiet time, whipping past a devo and some prayer as if I were in a fast-food drive-through. Rushing through my time alone with God made me spiritually smaller, weaker, and less satisfied. I felt more anxious and insecure. I had less compassion and patience. Even though I had technically had a quiet time, my life hadn't been changed in a meaningful way and—more significantly—even though I had been with God that morning, I wasn't honoring Him with the rest of my day.

Can you relate?

If you've ever felt tempted to zoom through your quiet time, let me encourage you to slow down and start learning today what took me a lot longer to figure out. You don't have to make the same mistakes I did in taking a fast-food approach to my time with God.

A major shift took place when I understood the words of 2 Corinthians 9:6: "Whoever sows sparingly will also reap sparingly, and whoever sows bountifully will also reap bountifully." A person who sows one seed will get a grand total of one plant. The person who sows hundreds of seeds . . . well, you get the picture. If we sow sparingly in our time with God, we'll reap sparingly in return. However, if we sow bountifully, the rewards will be *huge*! It's a no-brainer: if you want to experience a greater benefit from your time with God, you need to invest more into that relationship.

If you can ask yourself and answer the following two simple questions, you'll be way ahead of where I was for a long time:

1. How can I create more space in the day for my time alone with God?
2. How can I improve the quality of my quiet time?

Take a few minutes and write down at least two ideas in response to each question.

Go on.

Now, look back with me at our verses for today from Psalm 42. Note how excited the psalmist is to spend time with God. He literally cries out, "When can I go and meet with God?" Do you think your quiet time might be different if you had this kind of anticipation about your time alone with God? Yeah, me too.

The Bible tells us, "You do not have, because you do not ask" (James 4:2), so why don't you and I ask for a greater hunger for God and a greater excitement for spending time with Him? You ready for that?

READY TO GO DEEPER? Read Psalm 19:7–14. What does this passage teach us about God's Word? Spend some time giving thanks to God for each specific aspect of His Word described in Psalm 19.

No Filter

Let love be genuine. Abhor what is evil; hold fast to what is good.

Romans 12:9

It's honestly tough to know what's real these days. You watch a hilarious video online and then find out it was totally staged or edited. Fake news seems everywhere. People feel like they have to hashtag or caption "no filter" on social media photos because, otherwise, everyone will assume they've been doctored.

Maybe that's why Gen Z is so interested in authenticity. Like we mentioned previously, anyone under twenty-five years old falls into Gen Z, also called the "True Gen," a generation that wants to know what's real.[1] Do you ever get sick of wondering what's genuine? We do.

If you're under twenty-five, you probably don't remember a world without digital devices. You're a native to the world of both global connectivity and deep fakes. It's kind of head-spinning, to be honest. How do you navigate a world where things change in the time it takes to click a button?

Let us suggest something: hold on to what doesn't change. Anchor yourself to what's real, to what's lasting. Hebrews 13 declares an awesome truth: "Jesus Christ is the same yesterday and today and forever" (v. 8). You don't have to wonder if He's the "real thing."

Our verse for the day, Romans 12:9, gives us more insight. "Let love be genuine," God commands us. In other words, don't be fake in your relationships. Love people for real. The Bible tells us that God *is* love (1 John 4:7–8), so our love should be a reflection of the same yesterday, today, and forever God we serve.

We know it's not always easy to love people genuinely; relationships can be frustrating. We can't love authentically on our own. As God fills us with His love, though, we're able to deal with the challenging aspects of relationships without becoming unloving or fake in the process.

Some applications of this might be pretty obvious: Don't trash talk people. Choose kindness instead of selfishness. Learn to love something a person you care about loves, even if you don't initially understand why they feel that way. You may not get why someone is crazy about a band or a type of food, but when you show interest in what others are passionate about, you show them love on a deep level.

Other applications of the command to "let your love be genuine" aren't so simple. How do you love someone who's a fraud or an abuser? How do you show God's love to someone who's hurt you terribly? Jesus never says to pretend that it doesn't matter what people do or how they behave. Maybe that's why Romans 12:9 connects loving authentically to abhorring what's evil and clinging to what's good. This verse helps us understand what it means to hate the sin but love the sinner. Again, a simple statement that's pretty complicated to live out. That's why we need the never-changing, never-stopping, never-giving-up love and grace of Jesus. Let's hold fast to what is good, together. May our love be genuine today and always.

READY TO GO DEEPER? Read Hebrews 13:8–9. What kind of strange teachings might this verse be referring to? What might it look like for your heart to be strengthened by grace? Journal about it.

For Him and for You

I will not set before my eyes
anything that is worthless.
Psalm 101:3

Every once in a while, my husband (Zack) will hop on a video or share some thoughts for a blog at GirlDefined.com. Zack has great insight. It's always a treat to have him encourage the sisterhood, especially when it comes to understanding what to look for in a godly guy!

For one blog, I did a Q and A with Zack about romance, relationships, and red flags. I definitely think you'd benefit from checking it out. I'd like to bring up one tidbit today and reflect on what God's Word says about it. Zack wrote, "When it comes to red flags or cautions, I encourage you to dig beneath the surface and try to figure out who this guy really is (what are his passions, how does he spend his time, what does he watch when nobody is around, etc.). . . . Marrying a guy who is committed to moral purity says a lot about his character and how seriously he takes sin in his life."[1]

Zack's character gives me so much peace. I don't wonder whether my husband is trolling on nasty Internet sites. I'm not worried how Zack spends his time or money; I know he's pursuing Jesus. Of course, he's not perfect, but Zack committed himself to pursuing moral purity—mind, heart, and body—before I even met him, and he takes sin as seriously today as he did the day he first experienced the conviction of the Holy Spirit.

I'm not telling you all of this just to brag on Zack (even though he is pretty amazing). Instead, my intention is to urge you: don't settle for anything less than a guy who's "all in" with God. As his wife of almost ten years, I'm so thankful Zack decided to follow the verse from today's devotional:

> I will not set before my eyes
> anything that is worthless. (Ps. 101:3)

Sister, you and I both know there's a lot of worthless stuff out there. And many people are looking at it. It's a *major* red flag if a guy you're interested in views pornography on a regular basis. It's certainly not only guys who battle the lust of the eyes, though. Lots of us girls do as well. If viewing pornographic images or videos is a struggle for you, you're not alone. There's help and hope for breaking that cycle. I encourage you to get a copy of our book *Sex, Purity, and the Longings of a Girl's Heart* and search the archives on our blog at www.GirlDefined.com/archives to start your journey of healing.

However, you don't only have to be looking at porn to set worthless things before your eyes. Temptations to look at worthless things abound in our digital world. Just like we talked about in the devotional on thought life, you and I could spend entire days without ever actively choosing what to look at. If we just clicked on the next suggested video or meme that popped up on any of our feeds, we could endlessly look at things we didn't choose. And the reality is, a lot of those things are worthless.

Spend some time today journaling about this. Talk to God about what you hope for in a husband and also how your own viewing habits might change. I'm joining you in the fight to hold on to what is good, true, and beautiful.

READY TO GO DEEPER? Read Luke 11:34–36. How does this passage fit with what you read today? What "worthless" things might God be asking you to stop looking at? Pray for His help in choosing wisely.

DAY 57

Come On . . .

For am I now seeking the approval of man, or of God? Or am I trying to please man? If I were still trying to please man, I would not be a servant of Christ.

Galatians 1:10

Have you ever wanted to impress someone? Have you ever gone along with a conversation or laughed at a joke you didn't actually want to be part of? Have you ever done something you really didn't want to do, just because you didn't want to look stupid in front of your friends (or people you wanted to be your friends)? We totally have. We've given in to peer pressure, and most girls have or do at some point. Why? Because almost everyone cares what people—or at least *certain* people—think about them.

The Bible has a name for what fuels peer pressure: *the fear of man*. It's a weird-sounding phrase that many people haven't heard, so let's look at what it means. Hint: It doesn't mean hating males. It also doesn't mean hating mankind.

Do you remember the devotional on Day 51 that talked about the fear of the Lord? Since you learned that the fear of the Lord includes respecting God and longing for Him above everything else, taking God more seriously than anything and running to

Him instead of away from Him and to other things, what do you think the fear of man might mean?

Fear of man includes taking yourself and your status with other people more seriously than anything else. When we struggle with the fear of man, we respect (care about the opinion of) people more than the opinion of God. We long for the approval of others—maybe a certain crowd or a certain person—more than we seek God. Instead of running toward our loving Father, we run after whoever we're trying to impress. To sum up, fear of man keeps us back and holds us down in insecurity, whereas the fear of the Lord lifts us up in love.

We can hear some of you arguing with us in your heads, thinking, *I don't care what people think about me.* Okay. It's true that some people struggle less with the fear of man than others. But almost every single girl has *someone* she wants to impress. Perhaps you're intellectual and want your profs or teachers to approve of you. Or maybe you're a sporty girl who desires wins and trophies so people recognize how strong you are. Or you're a performer who longs to be noticed for your talents. Perhaps you're a "rule follower" who wants everyone to think you're *so* good. There's probably someone in your life who you fear (again, think of a person you respect more than anyone else and want the approval of, not that you're scared of them). Do you get where we're headed with this?

The apostle Paul acknowledged how devastating the fear of man can be. He straight-out says, "If I were still trying to please man, I would not be a servant of Christ" (Gal. 1:10). Does that seem a bit harsh to you? Think about it: If you fear man, can you honor Jesus above everyone else? You can't have it both ways.

Someone or some people will be at the top of your list. You can play for an audience of many or you can choose to honor an audience of one—the One who made you and loves you . . . forever.

Another of Jesus's disciples, Peter, addressed fear of man in Acts 5:29. He told the peers who were pressuring him, "We must obey God rather than men." *Must.* The only way forward is fear of the Lord, not fear of man. When you love Jesus more than anything else, you don't stop caring about people; you simply stop focusing on what they think about you. This frees you up to not only love God more but also love others more genuinely. When you're obsessed with what someone thinks about you, you're mostly thinking about *you.*

Ultimately this devotional is about something way bigger than not giving in to peer pressure. Even focusing on that will only get us so far. To be truly free, we need to cultivate our love for Jesus. Only His love can replace the fear of man in our minds and hearts. Spend some time today talking to God about this and asking Him to increase your love for Him. That's a prayer He loves to answer.

READY TO GO DEEPER? Read 1 John 4 using the Swedish Method. Now look back at verse 18. How does this fit with what you read today?

Burned Out

Come to me, all who labor and are heavy laden, and I will give you rest.

Matthew 11:28

You can't see, smell, or taste stress, but everyone feels it—and pretty regularly at that. Being stressed out affects even physically healthy people.

Have you ever been so stressed that you felt sick to your stomach? That uneasy, I-might-throw-up feeling has become so common for a lot of young adults that some think it's normal to be stressed out 24/7. Sister, that's not normal. Our world has simply accepted the abnormal and rebranded it.

Not too many years ago, some—but not all—high school graduates went on to higher education. Now it's assumed that students graduating high school will go on to college, and if you don't have a plan for your post-school life, people look at you with you're-going-to-end-up-living-in-your-parents'-basement pity. Okay, maybe they're not really thinking that, but the stress of being a young adult in today's day and age can be hard to deal with!

That's one reason Jesus's invitation in our verse for the day appeals so much: "Come to me, all who labor and are heavy laden, and I will give you rest" (Matt. 11:28). Many students and young career professionals are so routinely exhausted that when they have a moment to rest, they can't imagine doing anything beyond zoning out with their phones. Other people have no clue what it means to rest; they blaze from one activity to the next. A different kind of exhaustion stalks these friends.

If you've ever felt like life is too much to bear, that the weight you carry is too heavy for you, or if you've ever felt worn down by stress and exhausted by people's expectations of you, Jesus offers a different way forward. He invites you to find rest for your souls, to learn the unforced rhythms of grace. So many of us have pushed ourselves to the point that we don't know what it means to be "unforced." It's time to learn!

One of the ways we lean into and accept Jesus's invitation is by learning to listen to His voice more than any other. In the verses that follow Matthew 11:28, Jesus continues, "Take my yoke upon you, and learn from me, for I am gentle and lowly in heart, and you will find rest for your souls. For my yoke is easy, and my burden is light" (vv. 29–30). God doesn't put any weight on us that He won't help us bear if we seek Him. He doesn't have unrealistic expectations of us. He doesn't assume we have to do or be x, y, or z. He knows exactly who He created us to be, and He wants to help us thrive within His beautiful design. Psalm 16:11 promises that everlasting joy is found in God's presence. Not everlasting stress, not everlasting expectations.

When you listen to God's voice and follow where He leads you, you can leave stress behind. You're not "yoked" (burdened by, tied to) the world's expectations any longer. Jesus is gentle with you. You find rest for your soul. Doesn't that sound great?

We know it's not easy to silence the voices of our culture and even the voices in our own minds that tell us we have to be, do, act like, or want certain things. Those voices are often distorted by our sin nature and not in tune with God's Word. If you want to listen to God's voice, it will take an investment of your time, but it's so worth it. Both DesiringGod.org and TheGospelCoalition.org have some fantastic articles, videos, and podcasts that can help you tune in to God's voice through His written Word. Search "Listening to God," and you'll find a great place to start saying no to stress and yes to Jesus's invitation. You don't have to be weary and burdened any longer.

READY TO GO DEEPER? Read Luke 9:35. What does God command us to do in this verse? Is there a difference between hearing someone and listening to them? Journal about how listening to Jesus might impact your faith and your stress level.

DAY 59

Completely Free

And you will know the truth, and the truth will set you free.

John 8:32

The US Department of Justice recently released some shocking statistics. Approximately five out of six prisoners released from state jails return to prison within nine years. And 44 percent of those are rearrested during their first year after release, 68 percent within the first three years after being freed.[1] While other reasons for their return to incarceration certainly exist, one sad thing is apparent: some people struggle to stay permanently *free*. They return to harmful activities—selling drugs, committing petty thefts, hurting others—because they don't know life apart from crime.

In John 8:32, Jesus makes what we consider a pretty startling connection: "You will know the truth, and the truth will set you free." We don't know about you, but if someone asked us to say the first word we associated with freedom, it probably wouldn't be truth. For most people, freedom means not being ruled over or controlled. But Jesus is absolutely clear: it's truth that sets us free. Even truth that runs contrary to our feelings and opinions.

The Bible ties this theme together in other places. John 16:13 identifies God the Holy Spirit as the "Spirit of truth." Jesus calls

Himself "the way, and the *truth*, and the life" (John 14:6).² And 2 Corinthians 3:17 declares, "Where the Spirit of the Lord is, there is freedom." Wherever there is truth, there is freedom, because that's where God is.

How does this impact you, a twenty-first-century girl? You have a lot of choices to make, every day. But very few choices will be as important as this one: Will you live in truth? Sadly, truth is not the default setting of our brains. Our enemy is the father of lies. Ever since Adam and Eve believed the first lie in the garden, humans have been in bondage to deception: the "I'm not good enough" lies, the "I've got to take care of myself because no one else will" lies, the "It doesn't really matter if I do this one little thing" lies. They all keep us locked up in a prison of doubting our identity in Christ and doubting God's character and goodness. It may shock us that such a huge number of prisoners return to jail, but many of us don't know how to live in true freedom any more than they do. We may not be in literal chains, but we're in bondage, nonetheless. Only truth can set us free!

How can we actually live completely free? Since truth leads to freedom, we first need to learn how to discern between truth and lies. Before machines and markers existed to identify fake money, bankers were trained to recognize counterfeit bills. They didn't take classes in special techniques to spot fake dollars. Instead, they spent hours feeling real money. Their minds and their fingers became so accustomed to what real money felt like that they couldn't be fooled by counterfeit bills. You can probably see the connection here: if we want to *recognize* truth, we have to know it. We can't just learn to spot lies; we need to be so familiar with truth that lies will be obvious.

After we learn to discern between truth and lies, we must ruthlessly *reject* lies that try to worm their way into our thinking. Don't just recognize; reject! Maybe you hear the voice of accusation after looking in the mirror one morning: "You're so ugly. You're worthless, and nobody could ever love a girl like you." Reject that lie right away!

Next, you can *replace* any lie with truth from God's Word. In our example, you might replace the lie "I'm ugly" with "I'm precious, honored, and loved by God. God created me after His very image. He knitted me together and says I'm fearfully and wonderfully made" (Isa. 43:4; Gen. 1:26; Ps. 139:13–14).

Going through the recognize, reject, and replace steps may feel a little clunky at first, but it gets easier—like everything else— with practice. And what's waiting for you on the other side is *freedom*. Don't you think that's worth the effort? You don't have to be imprisoned by lies, sister. Chase after truth with us and stay completely free!

READY TO GO DEEPER? Read John 8:31–38. What else can you learn about freedom and truth from this passage? Journal about it, taking time to identify one lie you often believe and replacing it with truth.

DAY 60

An Ending and a Beginning

I have loved you with an everlasting love;
therefore I have continued my faithfulness to you.

Jeremiah 31:3

Sister, we are so proud of you. You've spent sixty days learning more about God and His Word. Way to go! You're shining brighter already! Whether you zipped right through this devotional or took a couple months doesn't matter to us; what matters is that you spent the time with Jesus. We're honored that you spent it with us too.

As we close this chapter in our time together, we want to leave you with some final encouragement. This doesn't have to be only an ending; it can also be a beginning, the start of an even closer walk with God.

C. S. Lewis wrote some amazing books, including The Chronicles of Narnia, a series of Christian allegorical books, which is a fancy way of saying they talk about Jesus by telling stories. Lewis's character Aslan represents Jesus, and Aslan's country represents heaven. In the final book of the Chronicles, *The Last Battle,* the world is ending and the faithful are being called into

Aslan's country. It might seem sad to think about the world ending and people dying, but *The Last Battle* paints a completely different picture.

In the final chapter, "Farewell to Shadowlands," Aslan welcomes his beloved ones to their perfect home. Lewis writes, "The things that began to happen after that were so great and beautiful that I cannot write them. . . . It was only the beginning of the real story. All their life in this world and all their adventures . . . had only been the cover and the title page: now at last they were beginning Chapter One of the Great Story which no one on earth has read: which goes on forever: in which every chapter is better than the one before."[1]

Girl, your life is part of an epic story, the Great Story. It's a story centered on Jesus and His everlasting love. It's a story of rescue from evil and of the promise that perfect fulfillment will come. That's what the whole Bible, Genesis through Revelation, promises. In Jeremiah 31:3, our verse for today, God declares this promise for the children of Israel:

> I have loved you with an everlasting love;
> therefore I have continued my faithfulness to you.

The God who faithfully loved His children then is the same God who faithfully loves His children today.

His love for you won't stop. He never gives up. We may have come to the end of our journey in this devotional, but His faithfulness to you will continue. The world may try to finesse you with lies that the Christian life is boring or that it's just a bunch of pointless, old-fashioned rules, but you can live in truth: your life is part of the most beautiful love story, the most riveting battle between good and evil ever known. And you know the end. Victory belongs to Jesus.

Just as we started this devotional with the love of God, we want to end there too. Don't forget how beloved you are, sister. When you know how loved you are, you can shine bright at school, work, home—wherever you are. God's love changes everything.

We wish we could give you a huge hug. We're sending one through these pages. Now, let's go live the rest of the story!

READY TO GO DEEPER? Read Psalm 42:1–2. Take a few minutes to pray these verses out loud. Remember that your relationship with God is where you will find the strength to shine bright for Him today, tomorrow, and every day to come.

Acknowledgments

God . . . thank You first and foremost for giving us the opportunity to write this devotional and proclaim Your goodness.

Zack and Dāv . . . our lifelong supporters and biggest fans. Thank you for being there for us, yet again! You never seem to grow weary of cheering us on, and we are grateful for that.

Our awesome families . . . thanks for always being there for us during each book-writing endeavor. Your prayers, words of encouragement, and overall interest in our books always give us the boost we need.

Jerusha Clark . . . thank you for going above and beyond to make this devotional a reality. You are a huge reason this book exists.

Rebekah Guzman . . . again, thank you for believing in us and giving us the opportunity to create this devotional. We can't thank you enough!

Patti Brinks . . . this cover is a dream come true. Thank you for working with us through all the ups and downs when we couldn't decide which cover we wanted. You are the best.

Baker Books . . . your team is incredible. We have truly loved working with every single person at Baker. Thank you for working with us to publish *Shine Bright*.

Friends who supported us along the way . . . thanks for sticking with us through yet another book.

Notes

Day 3 Love You to Life

1. Timothy Keller, *The Meaning of Marriage: Facing the Complexities of Commitment with the Wisdom of God* (New York: Penguin, 2013), 48.

Day 4 Finding Your Way

1. Adapted from Bethany Beal, "Understanding God's 'Road Map' for Your Womanhood," GirlDefined, accessed August 28, 2020, https://www.girldefined.com/understanding-gods-purpose-plan-womanhood.

Day 5 What Are You Afraid Of?

1. Mary Johnson, "Stress Levels Have Reached a 10-Year High among Adults in the US," July 15, 2019, https://www.bizjournals.com/washington/news/2019/07/15/stress-levels-have-reached-a-10-year-high-among.html.

2. Dr. Jeramy Clark and Jerusha Clark, *Your Teenager is Not Crazy: Understanding Your Teen's Brain Can Make You a Better Parent* (Grand Rapids: Baker Books, 2016), 204–12, 238–39.

3. Carmen P Mclean, "Brave Men and Timid Women? A Review of the Gender Difference in Fear and Anxiety," *Clinical Review Psychology* 29, no. 6 (July 2009): 496–505, https://www.researchgate.net/publication/26306175_Brave_men_and_timid_women_A_review_of_the_gender_difference_in_fear_and_anxiety; Jen DuBos, "Identifying the Three Fundamental Fears: Death, Abandonment, and Failure," Stenzel Clinical Services, accessed August 29, 2020, https://stenzelclinical.com/identifying-the-three-fundamental-fears-death-abandonment-and-failure/.

Day 6 Good, Good Father

1. New International Version.

Day 7 Would You Rather?

1. Adapted from Bethany Beal, "Strong Girls Desperately Needed to Stand Up for the Truth," GirlDefined, accessed August 30, 2020, https://www.girldefined.com /strong-girls-desperately-needed-stand-truth.

2. The Greek word *meno,* translated in John 15 as "abide" can also mean "dwell," as in living in a particular place. More available here: https://www.bereanbible church.org/transcripts/john/john_15_07-11_abiding-in-his-love.htm, accessed April 2, 2020.

3. Ephesians 1:19–20. See https://biblehub.com/greek/strongs_2904.htm for more detail.

Day 8 Not Some, But *All*

1. Adapted from Kristen Clark, "How to Deal with Secret Sexual Sin," GirlDe fined, accessed August 30, 2020, https://www.girldefined.com/how-to-deal-with -secret-sexual-struggles.

Day 10 What's in Your Heart?

1. See also Kristen Clark, "4 Easy-to-Miss Signs That You Struggle with Gossip," GirlDefined, accessed August 29, 2020, https://www.girldefined.com/4-easy -to-miss-signs-that-you-struggle-with-gossip.

2. New International Version.

Day 11 I'm Craving . . .

1. Faith Xue, "Craving Sugar? Your Body Is Probably Lacking This Nutrient," Byrdie, January 29, 2020, https://www.byrdie.com/what-do-sugar-cravings -mean; Kathryn Rubin, "Healthy Eating: What Your Food Cravings Mean," *Jerusalem Post,* June 15, 2011, https://www.jpost.com/health-and-science/healthy-eating -what-your-food-cravings-mean.

2. One suggestion is to use Bible Hub: https://biblehub.com/dictionary/.

Day 12 As We Forgive Those . . .

1. Adapted from Kristen Clark, "The Hardest Thing about Being a Christian Married Girl," GirlDefined, accessed August 29, 2020, https://www.girldefined .com/hardest-thing-christian-married-girl.

Day 16 What Are You Looking At?

1. Adapted from Kristen Clark, "Seduction: Using Feminine Allure in the Right Way," GirlDefined, accessed August 29, 2020, https://www.girldefined.com/seduction -using-feminine-allure-right-way.

Day 18 Check Your Blind Spot

1. *Dictionary.com*, s.v. "blind spot," accessed August 30, 2020, https://www.dictionary.com/brxowse/blind—spot?s=t.

Day 20 Run in Such a Way

1. Adapted from Bethany Beal, "How to Become a Woman Who Thrives," GirlDefined, accessed August 30, 2020, https://www.girldefined.com/how-to-become-a-woman-who-thrives.

Day 22 Your Outfit of the Day

1. *Dictionary.com*, s.v. "compassion," accessed September 1, 2020, https://www.dictionary.com/browse/compassion.

2. For more on this, check out B.B. Warfield, *The Emotional Life of Our Lord* (Ravenio Books, 2013), section 1, Kindle.

Day 24 The Gift No One Wants

1. Adapted from Bethany Beal, "The Secret to Achieving Diamond Status," GirlDefined, accessed September 1, 2020, https://www.girldefined.com/secret-achieving-diamond-status.

Day 25 The Secret to Better Friendships

1. Dale Carnegie, *How to Win Friends and Influence People* (New York: Pocket Books Edition, 1981), 52.

2. See https://www.girldefined.com/art-conversation-transformed-life.

3. See https://www.girldefined.com/how-to-build-friendships.

4. See https://www.girldefined.com/overcoming-social-fear-and-worry-ellissas-story.

Day 26 Scorched or Strong?

1. Adapted from Kristen Clark, "How to Nourish Your Soul on a Daily Basis," GirlDefined, accessed September 1, 2020, https://www.girldefined.com/nourish-soul-daily-basis.

Day 28 Friends Who Pick You Up

1. Adapted from Bethany Beal, "Tips for the Clumsy, Awkward, Self-Conscious Christian Girl," GirlDefined, accessed September 1, 2020, https://www.girldefined.com/tips-for-the-clumsy-awkward-self-conscious-christian-girl.

Day 30 Do the Next Right Thing

1. This and all verses used in today's devotional are taken from the New International Version.

Day 31 Therefore, I Have Hope

1. New International Version.

Day 32 A Game Changer

1. Adapted from Kristen Clark, "How I Found a Godly Woman to Mentor Me," Girl Defined, accessed September 1, 2020, https://www.girldefined.com/how-i-found-a-godly-woman-to-mentor-me; Bethany Beal, "What to Look for When Trying to Find a Mentor," GirlDefined, accessed September 1, 2020, https://www.girldefined.com/what-to-look-for-when-trying-to-find-a-mentor.

Day 34 Your Most Valuable Resource

1. Diogenes Laertius, *Lives of Eminent Philosophers*, ed. James Miller, trans. Pamela Mensch (New York: Oxford University Press, 2018), 413.

Day 36 Believe It or Not

1. Nancy Leigh DeMoss, *Choosing Gratitude: Your Journey to Joy* (Chicago: Moody Press, 2009), 23.

Day 38 Each of Us Is an Original

1. Erin Davis, "Best Of: But Why Can't I Look Like Her?" Lies Young Women Believe, January 2, 2013, https://liesyoungwomenbelieve.com/best-of-but-why-cant-i-look-like-her/.

2. Message.

Day 41 Better for You

1. *Merriam-Webster*, s.v. "quench," accessed September 2, 2020, https://www.merriam-webster.com/dictionary/quench.

Day 42 Worth the Wait

1. *Dictionary.com*, s.v. "wait," accessed September 2, 2020, https://www.dictionary.com/browse/wait?s=t.

Day 43 Can You Read?

1. Jen Wilkin, "Overcoming Bible Illiteracy," *Family Life Today*, March 9, 2015, https://www.familylife.com/podcast/familylife-today/overcoming-bible-illiteracy/.

2. Jen Wilkin, *Women of the Word: How to Study the Bible with Both Our Hearts and Our Minds* (Wheaton: Crossway, 2014).

Day 45 Good at What He Does

1. New International Version.

2. "The Sovereignty of God," DesiringGod, accessed September 2, 2020, https://www.desiringgod.org/topics/the-sovereignty-of-god.

Day 47 On Purpose

1. Dr. Barb Leonard, "What Is Life Purpose," University of Minnesota Taking Charge of Your Health and Wellbeing, accessed September 2, 2020, https://www.takingcharge.csh.umn.edu/what-life-purpose.

2. Tracy Francis and Fernanda Hoefel, "'True Gen': Generation Z and Its Implications for Companies," McKinsey & Company, November 12, 2018, https://www.mckinsey.com/industries/consumer-packaged-goods/our-insights/true-gen-generation-z-and-its-implications-for-companies.

3. Frederick Buechner, "Vocation," July 18, 2017, https://www.frederickbuechner.com/quote-of-the-day/2017/7/18/vocation.

Day 48 No Other Gods

1. Questions adapted from Timothy Keller, *Counterfeit Gods: The Empty Promises of Money, Sex, and Power, and the Only Hope that Matters* (New York: Dutton, 2009); and Kyle Idelman, *Gods at War: Defeating the Idols That Battle for Your Heart* (Grand Rapids: Zondervan, 2013).

2. Closing prayer taken from Psalm 51 and Exodus 20.

Day 49 Something Lost, Something Better Found

1. Adapted from Kristen Clark, "10 Signs Your Phone Is an Idol," GirlDefined, accessed September 4, 2020, https://www.girldefined.com/10-signs-phone-is-idol.

Day 51 The Kind of Fear That Leads to Life

1. Erik Thoennes and Jeremy Treat, "How to Have a Healthy Fear of God," *The Gospel Coalition Podcast*, July 23, 2019, https://www.thegospelcoalition.org/podcasts/tgc-podcast/healthy-fear-god/.

Day 52 The Right Kind of Influencer

1. New International Version.

Day 54 I Can't Wait

1. New International Version.

Day 55 No Filter

1. Francis and Hoefel, "'True Gen.'"

Day 56 For Him and for You

1. Kristen Clark, "Zack Answers Questions about Romance, Relationships, and Red Flags," accessed September 8, 2020, https://www.girldefined.com/zack-answers -questions-about-romance-relationships-and-red-flags.

Day 59 Completely Free

1. Dr. Mariel Alper, Matthew R. Durose, and Joshua Markman, "2018 Update on Prisoner Recidivism: A 9-Year Follow-Up Period (2005–2014)," May 23, 2018, https://www.bjs.gov/index.cfm?ty=pbdetail&iid=6266.

2. Emphasis added.

Day 60 An Ending and a Beginning

1. C. S. Lewis, *The Last Battle* (New York: HarperCollins, 2002), 228.

Kristen Clark is married to her best friend, Zack, and is the co-founder of GirlDefined Ministries. She is passionate about promoting the message of biblical womanhood through blogging, speaking, mentoring young women, and hosting Bible studies in her living room. In the end, she's just a fun-lovin' Texas girl who adores all things outdoors and drinks coffee whenever possible.

Bethany Beal is head over heels in love with her best friend and husband, David, and is the super proud mommy of Davey Jr. She is the cofounder of GirlDefined Ministries and is passionate about spreading the truth of biblical womanhood through writing, speaking, and mentoring young women. To her family and close friends, she is simply a tall blonde girl who is obsessed with iced lattes and can't get enough of her sweet baby, Davey Jr.

GirlDefined
MINISTRIES

Continue learning about
God's *incredible design*
for women . . .

GIRLDEFINED.COM

Listen to their new podcast,
The Girl Defined Show

▶ Girl Defined   🐦 @Girl_Defined

📷 @GirlDefined   📌 Girl Defined

f @GirlDefined   ✉ contact@girldefined.com

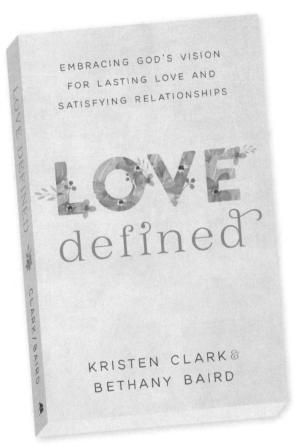

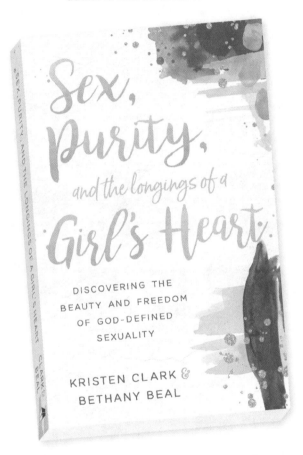